'John Henry Newman famously said ⸤...⸥ to have become perfect is to have ⸤...⸥ Murray may not be perfect, but he h⸤...⸥ open to change. It is this constant le⸤...⸥ his reflections on a lifetime of ministry so encouraging and helpful. He is currently a Baptist minister worshipping in an Anglican cathedral. He reflects generously on what he has received from the Church of England. This book returns the favour, giving Anglican clergy – and others – the opportunity to learn a lot from him. We need each other's wisdom to expand the scope and vision of Christian ministry. These 50 lessons from 50 years of ministry are a very good place to start.'

Rt Revd Stephen Cottrell, Archbishop of York

'Going the distance in ministry is the lifetime challenge for everyone who is called to expound God's Word and pastor God's People. Paul Beasley Murray has poured fifty years of his fruitful ministry experiences into this book and it provides wisdom, insight and practical encouragement for all engaged in the marathon of ministry.'

Revd David Coffey OBE, former President of the Baptist World Alliance

'The fruit of a life-time of ministry, this is vintage Beasley-Murray — accessible, passionate, full of wisdom about Christian ministry, and just occasionally, controversial. This is about ministry as it has been practiced over many years, and is not ashamed to reinforce the necessity of some practices that are in danger of being lost, such as pastoral visiting or careful preparation for worship by the minister (and not just delegated to the 'worship leader'.) For those embarking upon a life-time of ministry, this will help shape them for the tasks ahead, while for some of us with a few decades of ministry under our belts, it reminds us of what must not be lost, either in the rush to be 'relevant' or contemporary, or in the forgetfulness of retirement. Whether it is in commending the need to end a sermon well, or the vital necessity of a disciplined life of Scripture reading and personal prayer, Paul Beasley-Murray offers sound advice derived from personal experience. If only this had been available when I set out upon the life of ministry that has been my life for almost forty years! But then Paul's friendship over those decades ensured that much was offered personally. Now this is available to the widest of audiences, and many ministers will be grateful for that, and their congregations even more so.'

Revd Dr Paul Goodliff, General Secretary,
Churches Together in England

'A little over twenty years ago, as part of my exploration of a call to ordained Baptist ministry, I was charged to read a book entitled *Radical Believers* written by someone called Paul Beasley-Murray. Having been strongly influenced by his writing then, it is a privilege now to be invited to write a few words about this new book. Paul's experience is very different from my own – he is male, married, has always been in ministry and has served long pastorates in large churches – yet the topics he identifies and explores resonate strongly with my own experience, even when, sometimes, and shaped by our unique stories, we might differ in our reflection upon, and response to, them. Undergirded by extensive, up-to-date research and reading, this volume draws on a life-time of experience and has much to offer other ministers as they reflect on their own stories and spheres of service. Indeed, it has much to offer to those who are not ministers, providing insights into this most privileged, challenging and wonderful call to serve God and the people of God within a local church.'

Revd Catriona Gorton, Hillhead Baptist Church, Glasgow

'Ministers often search for the silver bullet – going to the next conference, listening to the next podcast, buying the next book – all in the hope of finding the elusive trigger to church growth and health. This is not the silver bullet – but is a helpful, practical, thoughtful and honest summary of some lessons and mistakes made by an experienced leader. Written by someone who has served in the trenches of the local church, it provokes and challenges while reassuring the reader that they are not alone – or the first to walk the path.'

Revd Canon David Richards,
St Paul's and St George's Church, Edinburgh

'With 50 years of pastoral experience to guide his insights, and a depth and breadth of reading that few can match, it is no surprise that Paul Beasley-Murray's latest book is filled with insight, wisdom and relevant guidance. The book is good humoured and accompanied by perceptive observations on both the timeless yet also changing face of ministry. A truly helpful gem.'

**Revd Dr Brian Harris, Principal,
Vose Seminary, Perth, Australia**

'As someone who was pastored by Paul for a decade, I can assure readers that he quite literally practices what he preaches. When I knew him as the minister of a large and busy church, he really did do all the things he writes about in this book. As an intern training for ministry I frequently argued with Paul about many of the principles and practices he outlines here. Once I had a bit more experience, I came to the conclusion that, in most cases, he had been right all along. I went into local church ministry with a set of very sound principles which have helped me time and again.'

Revd Emma Nash, accredited Baptist evangelist seconded to The Methodist Church's Evangelism and Growth Team

FIFTY LESSONS IN MINISTRY

With all good wishes

Paul Beasley-Murray

FIFTY LESSONS IN MINISTRY

REFLECTIONS ON FIFTY YEARS OF MINISTRY

Paul Beasley-Murray

DARTON·LONGMAN+TODD

First published in 2020 by
Darton, Longman and Todd Ltd
1 Spencer Court
140 – 142 Wandsworth High Street
London SW18 4JJ

Print book ISBN: 978-0-232-53468-9
eBook ISBN: 978-0-232-53469-6

A catalogue record for this book is available from the British Library

Phototypeset by Kerrypress, St Albans

Printed and bound by Bell & Bain, Glasgow

ACKNOWLEDGEMENTS

Unless otherwise indicated, Scripture quotations are from the New Revised Standard Version Bible, Anglicised edition, copyright © 1989, 1995 by the Division of Christian Education of the national Council of the Churches of Christ in the USA. Used by permission. All rights reserved.

Scripture quotations marked AV are taken from the Authorised Version of the Bible (The King James Bible), the rights in which are vested in the Crown, are reproduced by permission of the Crown's Patentee, Cambridge University Press.

Scripture quotations marked GNB are taken from the Good News Bible published by The Bible Societies/HarperCollins Publishers Ltd, UK © American Bible Society 1966, 1971, 1976, 1992, used with permission.

Scripture quotations marked NIV are taken from The Holy Bible, New International Version (Anglicised editi8on) copyright © 1979, 1984, 2011 by Biblica. Used by permission of Hodder & Stoughton Publishers, a Hachette UK company. All rights reserved.

I am grateful to be given permission by David Adam to quote from The Terminus which is published by Tim Tilney Ltd, Bristol BS6 5RR.

DEDICATION

For those ministers who worked alongside me in my churches in Altrincham and Chelmsford. I have been richly blessed with a succession of gifted men and women, who were great 'yoke fellows' (see Phil 4:3) – 'team mates' in modern jargon – in the service of Christ. It was because of their commitment – to God, the church, and to me – that we saw so much good happen.

Paul Cameron
David Grainger
Martin Hills
Glen Marshall
David Marson
Leesa McKay
Emma Nash
Matt Noble
Dave Richards
Matt Rowe
Mike Thornton
Nick Tuohy
Anne Wilkinson-Hayes

CONTENTS

A biographical note   xv
Introduction   xvii

1.   Ministry is rooted in the call of God   1
2.   Everybody needs the warmest of welcomes   5
3.   Names are important   9
4.   A multi-cultural church is a sign of the kingdom   13
5.   Evangelism is a process   17
6.   Transfer growth is a bonus, not a goal   21
7.   There is more to mission than making disciples   25
8.   The kingdom is not the church   29
9.   The key to pastoring is loving   33
10. Pastoral visiting has not had its day   37
11. Pastoral care requires organisation   41
12. Everyone is wounded   45
13. People need to be affirmed – constantly   49
14. Seniors also want to grow   53
15. Funerals are multi-faceted   57
16. Worship is both an art and a science   63
17. Spirit-led prayers in public worship are best prepared   67
18. Great worship climaxes around the Lord's Table   71
19. Good preaching entails structured simplicity   77
20. Sermon endings are key   81
21. Baptismal services provide great opportunities
     for gospel preaching   85
22. Every church is different   89
23. Meaningful fellowship is best expressed in small groups   93
24. Large is also beautiful   97
25. Church buildings matter   101

26. City and town-centre churches have a special role to play   105
27. Leaders make things happen   109
28. Teams empower God's people   113
29. Constant change is here to stay   117
30. Without a plan vision is only wishful thinking   123
31. Leadership demands passion   127
32. Communicate, communicate, communicate   131
33. The Spirit is no substitute for hard work   135
34. Brothers – and sisters – we are professionals!   139
35. A book a week keeps a minister awake   143
36. Annual reviews are to be welcomed   147
37. CMD is not an option   153
38. Ministers are made by their fellow leaders   157
39. Discipline is the other side of discipleship   161
40. Long pastorates have real advantages   165
41. Few churches are immune from power games   169
42. A soul friend encourages integrity   173
43. Monday morning blues are par for the course   177
44. Thank God for friends!   181
45. Thank God for family!   185
46. Ministry has its stages   191
47. Retirement marks a major new stage in ministry   195
48. Never give up   199
49. Ministry is tough but rewarding   203
50. Ministry is rooted in the grace of God   207

Appendix   211

BIOGRAPHICAL NOTE

Paul Beasley-Murray was born on 14 March 1944. He read Modern Languages (French and German) and Theology at Jesus College, Cambridge. While completing a PhD in New Testament studies at Manchester University, he trained for the ministry at the Northern Baptist College, Manchester, and at the International Baptist Theological Seminary in Rüschlikon-Zurich. Ordained on 10 October 1970, he served with the Baptist Missionary Society in Congo/Zaire, where he taught New Testament and Greek in the Protestant Theological Faculty of the National University (1970-1972). Paul pastored two churches: Altrincham Baptist Church, Cheshire (1973-1986) and Central Baptist Church, Chelmsford, Essex (1993-2014). He was also Principal of Spurgeon's College, London (1986-1992).

Paul now worships at Chelmsford Cathedral, and is involved in their Sunday 'Breakfast with the Bible' programme, as well as leading a home group. He still retains his Baptist roots: he chairs the College of Baptist Ministers and leads a fellowship for retired ministers in Mid- and South Essex, which he helped to found.

He continues to be a patron of the Society of Mary and Martha, a retreat centre based at Sheldon, near Exeter, he is also a patron of the J's Young Adults Hospice which is part of the Essex-based Havens Hospices. He has been president of the Rotary Club of Chelmsford Rivermead, and in 2018 was made a Paul Harris fellow. In 2019 he became Chairman of the Cambridge Society of Essex, an alumni association.

Throughout his ministry Paul has been a prolific author. In retirement Paul has published a four-volume guide to ministry, *Living Out the Call* (Feed-a-Read 2015; revised 2016); updated two booklets on pastoral care, *A Loved One Dies: Help in the first few weeks* and *Happy Ever After? A workbook for couples preparing for marriage* (College of Baptist Ministers 2017); edited eight volumes (520 articles) of *Ministry Today UK: 1994-2018* (College of Baptist Ministers, 2018); written his autobiography; *This is my story: a story of life, faith, and ministry* (Wipf & Stock 2018) as also *Make the Most of Retirement* (BRF 2020), a guide primarily for ministers. He has engaged in three research projects, which resulted in an 8000-word article on 'The reading habits of ministers' (*Baptist Quarterly* 49, January 2018); *Retirement Matters for Ministers: A report into a research project into how Baptist ministers experience retirement* (College of Baptist Ministers, 2018); and *Entering New Territory. Why are retired Baptist ministers moving to Anglican churches? What are the underlying theological issues?* (College of Baptist Ministers, 2019). Together with Terry Calkin he has written for pastors in the developing world four short books on *The Four Foundations of Leadership* which await publishing. Every Thursday he also posts a blog relating to *Church Matters*.

Married to Caroline, HM Senior Coroner for Essex and a past President of the Coroners Society of England and Wales, they have four married children. In addition to their eight grandchildren, his interests include cooking, travel and parties. See further www.paulbeasleymurray.com

INTRODUCTION

I was ordained to the Christian ministry on Saturday 10 October 1970 at Holmesdale Road Baptist Church, South Norwood, London SE 25. On Sunday 11 October 2020 I will celebrate the fiftieth anniversary of my ordination at a special service of Evensong in Chelmsford Cathedral. *Fifty Lessons in Ministry: Reflections on Fifty Years of Ministry* has been published to celebrate that anniversary.

Ministry has changed enormously in the past fifty years – and inevitably I too have changed in my approach to ministry. One of the things I have enjoyed throughout my ministry is rising to the challenge of learning new ways of serving God and his people. Even in retirement I have not stopped learning: indeed, one of the joys of worshipping in Chelmsford Cathedral has been to explore new ways of doing church and of worshipping God, and in the process I have continued to grow and develop in my journey with Christ. *Fifty Lessons in Ministry* is a record of some of the lessons I have learnt over the past fifty years.

Although books on ministry abound, I am not aware of another book quite like this where an experienced minister looks back over fifty years of ministry with a view to 'passing on the baton' to others. When I started to write this book, I had in mind particularly ministers in training. As a result of sharing some of these lessons with experienced ministers, I now dare to believe that the book will be of interest to ministers in general, as also to many other church people too. Furthermore, although these lessons were learnt primarily within the context of Baptist churches, I am convinced that most, if not all, the lessons are applicable to ministry within a variety of denominational and theological contexts.

Finally, those who are familiar with earlier writings, will see that, inevitably, some of the reflections recorded here are a development of my thinking found in previous books[1] and blogs.[2] Nonetheless, *Fifty Lessons in Ministry* is very much a new book, precisely because learning for me has always been an ongoing process.[3]

---

[1] See in particular Paul Beasley-Murray, *Living out the Call: 1. Living to God's Glory; 2. Leading God's Church; 3. Reaching God's World; 4. Serving God's People.* Feed-a-Read 2015; revised in 2016.

[2] I write a weekly blog entitled *Church Matters*: see www.paulbeasleymurray.com

[3] Although I had previously drawn up a list of headings denoting lessons learnt in the course of 43 years of ministry, that list is significantly different from the lessons I elaborate here: see *Living Out the Call: 1. Living for God's Glory*, 23-24.

MINISTRY IS ROOTED IN THE CALL OF GOD

Just as there is no stereotyped conversion experience, so too there is no fixed pattern of call. Donald Coggan, a former Archbishop of Canterbury, reflecting on the Apostle Paul's dramatic conversion experience on the Damascus Road, when God also called Paul to serve him as an apostle to the Gentiles, made the wise comment: 'God has as many ways of reaching our innermost beings with his love as he has of giving us different faces or different finger-prints … Let us remember that, as there is a mystery surrounding the Being of God, so there is a mystery at the heart of his ways with men. Perhaps above every story of conversion we should write the warning: "Mystery! God at work!".'[1] Michael Ramsey, another former Archbishop of Canterbury, similarly wrote of the different ways God calls people: 'To some there may be an overwhelming sense of divine impressing upon the conscience. To others, the call may be one which stirs the mind to deep and enquiring thought. To others the call may be to the feeling of compassion for one's fellows in the world, a compassion shared with the compassion of God.'[2]

In my own case, brought up within a Christian home, there was never a time when I did not believe that God had called me to be a minister. I wish I could say that it was otherwise. I wish I could not have been so open to the charge of following in steps of my father. But the fact is that like Isaiah's Servant of the Lord (Isa 49:1), Jeremiah the prophet (Jer. 1:5) and Paul the apostle (Gal. 1:15), I have been conscious of God's hand upon my life from the very beginning of days. True, as a teenager at one stage I sought to make

---

[1] Donald Coggan, *Paul: Portrait of a Revolutionary* (London, Hodder & Stoughton, 1984), 36, 37.
[2] A. M. Ramsey, *The Christian Priest Today* (London, SPCK, 2nd edn., 1985), 101.

a half-hearted struggle against it, but I quickly gave up. If there was one text which summed up my call to ministry, it was some words of Jeremiah: 'If I say, 'I will not mention him, or speak any more in his name', then within me there is something like a burning fire shut up in my bones; I am weary with holding it in, and I cannot' (Jer. 20:9). For me ministry was not one option among many: I felt I had never had any other choice. God had laid his hand upon me and there was no escape. God had called me to ministry – and, in particular, God had called me to preach.

This sense of call has sustained me and acted as a sheet-anchor when difficulties have come my way. In the words of the Apostle Paul: 'An obligation is laid on me, and woe to me if I preach not the Gospel' (1 Cor. 9:16). Or, in the words of Martin Luther: 'Here I stand, I can do no other'. My security was not to be found in the fact that the church had to give me nine months' notice if it wished to dismiss me, but that God had laid his hand on me and called me to be his minister.

The church may have paid me a stipend, but the church never owned me. In the eyes of Her Majesty's Revenue and Customs I may have been employed, but in the eyes of the law, and above all in the sight of God, I was accountable to God alone (see Heb. 13:17). Like the Apostle Paul I had been 'sent neither by human commission nor from human authorities, but through Jesus Christ and God the Father' (Gal. 1:1). This is a frightening, but also a liberating thought. It means that, ultimately, I am not dependent upon what others may think of me. It is not other people's judgement which counts, but God's.

My call to ministry gave me security. True, there is an inevitable degree of subjectivity in the call. A call is always an inward experience. It is an affair of the heart involving only God and the individual concerned. It is an inner conviction arising from a sense that God has laid hold of me – even 'overpowered' me (Jer. 20:7). I could not in any way prove scientifically my sense of call. All I know is that I did not volunteer, rather I responded: 'Here am I; send me' (Isa. 6:8).

Yet, having said that, there was an objective side to my calling, for the genuineness of my call had been tested by God's people and found not to be wanting. The act of ordination on 10 October

1970 was the church's public recognition of the rightness of my response. As is the norm amongst British Baptists, my ordination took place in my 'sending' church, South Norwood Baptist Church (Holmesdale Road) in South London. As also tends to be the case, I was the only person to be ordained on that occasion. Unusually, I was ordained as a missionary with the charge to 'go and make disciples of all nations' (Matt. 28:19): indeed within three days of that service Caroline and I were on our way to the Congo (we travelled to Antwerp, where we set sail for Matadi, the port of Congo). The service was led by my minister, Donald Monkcom, who had served with the Baptist Missionary Society (BMS) in Jamaica; the ordination was conducted by Fred Drake, the Associate Overseas Secretary of the BMS with special responsibility for Africa, the West Indies, and Brazil. The sermon was preached by my father, then the Principal of Spurgeon's College. Those who set me apart by laying hands on me included not just Donald Monkcom, Fred Drake and my father, but also Robert Morrison, the Church Secretary of my sending church (Baptists always have at least one non-ordained person to take part in the laying-on-of-hands) and Jack Swanson, the minister of the Baptist Church in Chorlton-cum-Hardy, to whom I had been assigned while training for the ministry in Manchester.

I find it significant that with the passing of the years my ordination has gained increased importance for me. At the time there had been so many other pressing things on the go. In the first place, there was the culmination of my academic studies in my application for the degree of Doctor of Philosophy (PhD). I had submitted my thesis in the June of 1970, but the actual *viva* (oral examination) did not take place until the September. Secondly, because I was due to teach Greek and New Testament in the medium of French in the Congo, the time between my PhD submission and my ordination was dominated first by going on a three-week Berlitz course to brush up my spoken French and secondly by the writing of some of my initial lectures in French. Thirdly, because we were due to depart for the Congo just three days after my ordination, we were preparing for a new life with the BMS in the Congo – undergoing medical check-ups, starting on anti-malaria pills, having jabs for diseases like yellow fever, buying mosquito nets, water filters and lightweight clothing, as well as a lot of staple food. In this context ordination was but one of many significant events happening to me. Unlike Anglican ordinations which are normally immediately preceded by a retreat, there was no spiritual build-up to my ordination – it just happened! Consequently, at the time my ordination did not stand out for me: I did not 'feel' it to be spiritual high. Yet, as I state in my 'CV' on my website it was one of the four major events in my life: the first was my birth on 14 March 1944 in Ilford, a suburb in East London (at the time in Essex); the second was my baptism on 17 November 1957 in Zurich (Salemskapelle); the third was my wedding on 26 August 1967 in Wrexham (The Old Meeting); and the fourth was my ordination on 10 October 1970.

In summary, my ministry has been rooted in my sense of call, confirmed by God's people in the act of ordination. What is true of me is surely true of all ministers of the Gospel.[3]

---

[3] See Paul Beasley-Murray, 'Ordination in the New Testament' 1-13 and 'The Ministry of All and the Leadership of Some' in Paul Beasley-Murray (ed.), *Anyone for Ordination* (MARC, Tunbridge Wells 1993).

EVERYBODY NEEDS THE WARMEST OF WELCOMES

As a young couple Caroline and I had a bad experience of church. It happened while we were missionaries in Congo. I had been invited to give some lectures at an Anglican college just outside Nairobi. Our hosts offered to look after our two young children so that we could attend church in Nairobi. We were so excited, not least because we had not attended an English-language service for eighteen months. As we entered the church we sensed the vibrancy of this large congregation, but nobody spoke to us – neither before nor after the service. We sat there, longing for somebody to come up to us, but nobody did. They were all too busy chatting to one another. They failed to notice this lonely young couple, and as a result our loneliness was intensified. Perhaps we should have made an effort to speak to others – but at the time we felt low spiritually and hadn't the energy. We left feeling utterly depressed. From that time on, I determined that nobody would be able to visit a church of which I was the minister without getting a welcome. Everybody needs the warmest of welcomes.

But how does that translate into action? In the first place the welcome begins at the door of the church. Nobody must be able to slip into a church without receiving a personal welcome. In that regard I remember an occasion when, on sabbatical, I visited a church in another town. As I entered there was a woman at the door who had been given the task of welcoming visitors that Sunday morning – but she did not ask my name. Nor did she think of showing me how to access the worship area, let alone showing me to a seat. I passed people happily talking to one another, but nobody talked to me. Nobody took any notice of me, even when

I sat down with people either side of me! As I awaited the start of the service I read in the church news-bulletin that 'if you are visiting with us today, we are glad to have you here'. Yet at no point was that welcome personalised. It was not as if it were a big church, where I could be lost in the crowd. I counted the heads – there were 62 of us (including the children). It was a thoroughly disheartening experience of church. However, I have little doubt that the church would have regarded itself as a welcoming church. After all, they did have in the pews a welcome slip, which I would have filled in had there been a pen – and had I known to whom the slip should have been given! But the church was not actively looking out for visitors; instead, the members were focussed on one another. I found the failure of a church to offer a personal welcome unforgiveable. A genuine 'Jesus community' must surely be 'warm and welcoming'. To be warm and welcoming means that the church needs to discover the names of their visitors. I believe that had Jesus been standing at the door of that church, he would not have just said to me 'Good morning', but 'Good morning, Paul'. Jesus, the Good Shepherd, 'calls his own sheep by name' (John 10:3) – and so too should we!

In larger churches, one person standing at the door is not sufficient. A welcoming team is needed, whose task is to give a personal welcome, to get alongside newcomers and to introduce them to others. Members of such a team must be outgoing people, with a passion to make newcomers feel at home. They also must be committed to being on duty every Sunday. As John Truscott, an experienced church consultant, rightly said:

> This is specialised work. It cannot be done well by different home groups, or any system that involves a rota. It needs the same people on week by week – so last week's (or, more likely, last month's) newcomer is recognised and welcomed by name this week. Better to have a team of five dedicated people who make it their priority than to share it round a larger number.[1]

---

[1] See John Truscott, *Creative Organisation for Effective Ministry*: 'Test for your Church Welcome' (August 2018).

To this I would add that every member of the welcome team needs to be committed to arriving early and leaving late, as also to remembering the names and not just the faces of their visitors. In the end I came to feel so strongly about welcoming people that I did away with the custom of meeting my leaders just before the service to pray for God to bless the service. Instead we moved that time of prayer half an hour earlier, so that all of us could be involved in welcoming people to church. Furthermore, when we came to redevelop our buildings in Chelmsford, I ensured that there was just one way in and one way out. Then on Sundays I became the 'gatekeeper' (see John 10:9), and would stand at the door so that nobody could enter or leave church without being greeted by me!

However, an initial welcome at the door is not enough. Everybody needs to be motivated to look out for newcomers. I constantly challenged people to get to know 'one new name each Sunday'. I wanted a welcoming spirit to be written into the church's DNA. In this regard Lawrence Peers told of a large urban American church which began to grow once the members of the church agreed to use the first half-hour after the worship service to 'be present' to their visitors – that 'intentional first half hour' made all the difference.[2] It has been rightly said that: 'The most important element of being a more welcoming church is a commitment from the whole congregation to be more welcoming. Although welcoming procedures are important, a welcoming attitude is vital.'[3]

To encourage a welcoming attitude in the church I once preached a sermon in which I said: 'I long to be the pastor of the friendliest church I town. I long for my church to be the most open, the most accepting, the most caring, the most supportive, and the most loving church in town'. After the service a church member came up and criticised me for encouraging our church to compete with other churches. I replied, 'Wouldn't it be great if all the churches in our town were to seek to be the friendliest church in town!'

---

[2] Lawrence Peers, 'What it takes to make congregational change stick', *Alban Conversation* 16/07/2007.
[3] Rob Norman, quoted in Steve Chalke with Sue Radford, *New Era, New Church?* (HarperCollins, London, 1999), 10.

Finally, do note that a welcome doesn't end when everybody has gone home. The welcome needs to be reinforced by following up the visit. At the very least, a letter – personally addressed and personally signed by the minister – needs to be put in the post saying how pleased the church was to see them. If the newcomers have just moved into town, send flowers with a card welcoming them to the area. Best of all is a personal visit by the minister – that was always one of my key responsibilities. True, in a larger church where there are visitors every Sunday this can be demanding. As a result, I used to wait and see if the visitors returned the following Sunday: if so, then I made an appointment to go and visit them.

To sum up, everybody needs the warmest of welcomes!

NAMES ARE IMPORTANT

One of the most fascinating chapters in the New Testament is Romans 16. Yet at first sight it is one of the most boring of chapters, for it is largely a list of names. Here Paul greets twenty-six individuals by name:

> Greet Prisca and Aquila, who work with me in Christ Jesus, and who risked their necks for my life, to whom not only I give thanks, but also all the churches of the Gentiles. Greet also the church in their house. Greet my beloved Epaenetus, who was the first convert in Asia for Christ. Greet Mary, who has worked very hard among you. Greet Andronicus and Junia, my relatives who were in prison with me; they are prominent among the apostles, and they were in Christ before I was. Greet Ampliatus, my beloved in the Lord. Greet Urbanus, our co-worker in Christ, and my beloved Stachys. Greet Apelles, who is approved in Christ. Greet those who belong to the family of Aristobulus. Greet my relative Herodion. Greet those in the Lord who belong to the family of Narcissus. Greet those workers in the Lord, Tryphaena and Tryphosa. Greet the beloved Persis, who has worked hard in the Lord. Greet Rufus, chosen in the Lord; and greet his mother—a mother to me also. Greet Asyncritus, Phlegon, Hermes, Patrobas, Hermas, and the brothers and sisters who are with them. Greet Philologus, Julia, Nereus and his sister, and Olympas, and all the saints who are with them. Greet one another with a holy kiss. All the churches of Christ greet you. (Rom. 16:3-16)

Of what possible interest, some might say, can these verses be – apart perhaps from some keen Christian parents looking for a 'biblical' name for a child? Yet in many ways it is a highly

instructive list of names. For instance, of the twenty-six named
individuals nine are women and seventeen are men, but more
women than men are commended for being active in the church –
what has changed! Furthermore, only three of the twenty-six can
be positively identified as Jews; fourteen appear not to have been
born in Rome itself and were 'immigrants'. A study of the names
also shows that some two-thirds of those mentioned were probably
slaves. The church in Rome was an amazing cultural mix.[1]

Even more significant, said the great Swiss theologian Emil
Brunner, this list comes at the end of 'the greatest, the richest and
hardest piece of doctrinal writing in the whole Bible'.[2] It is the
one and the same Paul who penned the fifteen preceding chapters
and this sixteenth chapter. From this Brunner drew the fascinating
conclusion:

> The Christian Community consists of persons, and the
> most important, indeed the only thing in the Community
> that matters are persons, and the most important, indeed,
> the only thing in the Community that matters are persons:
> God, Jesus Christ, the Holy Spirit and Christian people. The
> relationship of these persons to one another – that alone is
> essential in the Christian Community; it does not concern
> things or doctrines in themselves.[3]

There is another important aspect to this list of twenty-six people:
Paul greeted so many by name. Even in a church Paul had yet to
visit, he knew twenty-six people. I wonder, did Paul realise the
significance of greeting people by name? Did he know how powerful
that is? According to Dale Carnegie, an American famous for courses
on self-improvement and salesmanship 'A person's name is to him
or her the sweetest and most important sound in any language'.[4]
Similarly, Joyce Russell, an American 'business coach' wrote:

> A person's name is the greatest connection to their own
> identity and individuality. Some might say it is the most
> important word in the world to that person. It is the one way

---

[1] See Colin G. Kruse, *Paul's Letter to the Romans* (Apollos, Nottingham, 2012) 574-575.
[2] Emil Brunner, *The Letter to the Romans: Commentary* (Lutterworth, London, 1959) 126.
[3] Brunner, *The Letter to the Romans*, 126.
[4] Dale Carnegie, *How to Win Friends and Influence People* (Simon & Schuster, New York, 1936).

we can easily get someone's attention. It is a sign of courtesy and a way of recognising them. When someone remembers our name after meeting us, we feel respected.'[5]

To greet people by name shows that we value them – they count. For me one of the most wonderful verses in the Bible is John 10:3, where Jesus says that the Good Shepherd 'calls his own sheep by name'. What a difference those words make to me. Whereas agencies such as the National Health Service and Her Majesty's Revenue & Customs know me primarily as a number, Jesus knows me by name. He values me. He loves me. In turn we too are called to love one another and value one another by knowing one another by name. Names are important and for that reason we too should greet our fellow brothers and sisters in Christ by name. It is not enough to say on a Sunday morning, 'Hi, how are you?' Superficiality may be sufficient in the everyday world, but not amongst God's people. We need to be able to address one another by name.

'That's fine in a small church with a dozen people,' some might say, 'but in our church with 120 members that is impossible.' I disagree. I am convinced that when English people say they have a bad memory for names, by and large they are not telling the truth. What in effect they are saying is, 'I can't be bothered; I am too lazy.' The proof of this is to compare English people with Americans. It is rare for an American to forget a person's name. In American culture knowing a person's name is important, and so Americans tend to make a real effort to remember names. It is not that they are any cleverer than us – it is that in this respect they are more determined.

How many names can we expect to know? Without effort probably most people can remember at least 150 people by name.[6] – but with application we can know many more. I read of an

---

[5] *Washington Post*, 20 January 2014.
[6] According to Oxford anthropologist, Robin Dunbar, 150 is the number of people with whom we can maintain a meaning relationship: see Christine Ro, 'Dunbar's number: why we can only maintain 150 relationships', *BBC Future*, 9 October 2019. This is in line with the findings of a survey of 350 Baptist churches where Alan Wilkinson and I discovered that 'A full time pastor could cope with the demands of a growing church with a membership of under 150. But that beyond that point the strain and limitations begin to have an adverse effect on the potential growth of the church' (*Turning the Tide*, Bible Society, London, 1981), 57.

American mega-church pastor who claimed to know all 16,000 of his members by name.

What's the secret? Probably, in the first place, by showing more interest in the people we meet. It often helps to repeat a person's name. In my case, I always have some cards in my jacket – and I immediately write down the names of people I do not know. When I get home, I write up the names and the conversation. Although no longer a pastor of a church, I have a file on my computer in which I list names, addresses, and salient information about people I meet. As far as I am aware, this private list is not covered by data protection!

Of course, there are ways in which we can help one another. Some churches expect their members – including the minister(s) – to wear name badges every Sunday. That is what happens at Rotary: at every meeting members are expected to turn up with their name badge. If that seems over the top, then what about having a regular (once every three or four months?) 'name-tag Sunday' when everybody attending the service is asked to fill in their name on a badge or on a sticky label?

The fact is that names are important, for people are important.

A MULTI-CULTURAL CHURCH IS A SIGN OF THE KINGDOM

As a young minister I was attracted by the writings of Donald McGavran and Peter Wagner into how churches grow. I longed to see my church grow and develop and felt that the American church growth movement of the 1970s had something to offer British churches. However, although I learnt much from them, I came to realise that their promotion of what they termed 'the homogeneous principle' was a denial of the Gospel.

Let me explain. A homogeneous unit is 'a section of society whose common characteristic is a culture or a language'.[1] Or to put it more simply, 'birds of a feather flock together'. Like attracts like. Donald McGavran, the father of the church growth movement, observed that 'people like to become Christians without crossing racial, linguistic or class barriers'.[2] Up to that point I was, and still am, with McGavran. In my judgment there is no reason why we cannot use the homogeneous unit principle in evangelism.[3] Indeed, to a degree that happens in every church: young people reach out to young people, older people to older people, women to women, and men to men. By extension we could justify black Africans reaching out to black Africans, Arabs to Arabs, Asians to Asians. Perhaps more controversially, we could justify people of different socio-economic classes reaching out to their peers. But

---

[1] Donald McGavran, *Understanding Church Growth* (Eerdmans, Grand Rapids, 2nd edition, 1973), 85.

[2] McGavran, *Understanding Church Growth*, 199.

[3] Similarly Peter Cotterell, *Church Alive* (IVP, Leicester, 1981) 40: 'The homogeneous unit ... is a reality. It is necessarily found in unredeemed society, and since evangelism must take place in unredeemed society, it is apparent that evangelism ought to take note of the role of the homogeneous unit ... But when people become Christians, when they join a local congregation, they have to learn a new way of life. They must learn biblical ideas which are not exclusive. In the church all are welcome.'

a major theological difficulty arises when Donald McGavran and Peter Wagner go the next step and argue for the creation of 'one-people' churches.

So, for instance, Peter Wagner used the homogeneous principle as one of his seven 'vital signs' of a healthy growing church. He stated: 'The membership of a healthy growing church is composed basically of one kind of people.'[4] Although McGavran denied it, this is segregation – or certainly it is perceived as segregation.[5] The tragedy of the American church is that the most segregated day and time within a week is Sunday morning at 11 o'clock. Inevitably some churches are homogeneous, for the simple reason that they are ministering in an area where everybody comes from the same background. However, to promote the homogeneous church as an ideal cannot be right, even if the principle may appear to 'work'. Churches by definition are places where everybody is welcome. In the words of the Apostle Paul, 'There is neither Jew nor Greek, slave nor free, male nor female, for we are all one in Christ Jesus' (Gal. 3:28). In the light of this, Jürgen Moltmann declared: 'National churches, racial churches, class churches, middle class churches, are in their practical life heathenish and heretical.' He went on, to reflect the will of God a community must consist of 'the unlike, of the educated and uneducated, of black and white, of the high and the low'.[6] Moltmann was right. The glory of the church is our unity in diversity. It is this unity which is a sign of the in-breaking of the Kingdom. In Britain's multi-cultural cities and towns, a church which deliberately sets out to be made up of one group of people runs counter to the very essence of the Kingdom. We are called to live the Kingdom in our life together for, in the words of Lesslie Newbigin, 'the only hermeneutic of the gospel is a congregation of men and women who believe it and live by it'.[7]

When I was a minister in Altrincham, apart from the Jewish community, the town was very much mono-cultural. When I

[4] C. Peter Wagner, *Your Church Can Grow: Seven Vital Signs of a Healthy Growing Church* (Regal, Glendale, California, 1976), 110.

[5] According to McGavran, *Understanding Church Growth*, 211: 'Segregation is a sin because it is an exclusion enforced by one group on another. "One-people" churches are not, since they are the choice of a group as to language and customs and do not come about through a desire to exclude "inferiors" – quite the contrary.'

[6] Jürgen Moltmann, *The Gospel of Liberation* (Waco, Word, 1973), 91.

[7] Lesslie Newbigin, *The Gospel in a Pluralist Society* (London, SPCK, 1989), 227.

arrived in Chelmsford the town was also almost exclusively mono-cultural. However, around the year 2000 the make-up of Chelmsford began to change, and we went all out to welcome Africans – and people of other ethnic groups too. Eventually about one hundred people associated with our church came from other cultures. We held many international evenings, celebrating our diversity in Christ. However, the real challenge we faced was not just to welcome, but to integrate our new friends. On 23 April 2008 Wale Hudson-Roberts, the Racial Justice Coordinator of the Baptist Union of Great Britain, met with some of us, and asked: 'Are you a multi-ethnic church (i.e. a church made up of people from different cultures, but who do not relate to one another) or are you a genuinely multi-cultural church (i.e. a church made up of people from different cultures who do relate to one another)?' In my notes I wrote: 'We agreed we were on the way to becoming a multi-cultural church, but acknowledged we had a long way to go. We reflected on the insecurity that people from minority cultures experience and asked ourselves how people from minority cultures could really be themselves in our church.'

The fact is that difference and diversity in the church are not always easy to handle. It is easy to misunderstand one another. It is easy too to ignore one another. Yet we need to reach out to one another more. It is not enough to be fellow-worshippers – we need to get to know one another, understand one another, and become friends of one another. Indeed, Paul says that we should *honour* (1 Cor. 12:24) those who *'seem to be weaker'* (1 Cor. 12:22): i.e. we need to affirm those who feel of less value than others. In a multi-cultural church where whites are in the majority, it is not easy belonging to the minority. How do we affirm those who belong to a different culture? Paul seems to suggest that there is a place for positive discrimination. Goodness, what would that look like?

In retirement I now worship at Chelmsford Cathedral. In the five or so years we have been there we have seen a noticeable increase in the number of African and Asian Christians present at the Sunday services. Sadly, like so many other churches, the Cathedral has yet to become a multi-cultural church: that is a journey still to be made. However, it is a journey that needs to be made. It cannot be right that at this stage of Chelmsford's development only white

Anglo-Saxons serve the bread and wine in its Cathedral.

This challenge to engage with a diversity of culture was something the early church had to face. The question, for instance, which the Council of Jerusalem had to consider was did Gentile Christians have effectively to adopt a Jewish culture in order to become full members of the church of God? I note with interest that in Antioch the leadership of the church was surprisingly diverse and multi-ethnic (see Acts 13:1). Barnabas was from Cyprus; Simon called Niger was almost certainly an African, for Niger is a Latinism meaning 'black'; Lucius of Cyrene came from North Africa; Manaen was a man of some considerable social standing for he was 'a member of the court of Herod'; and Paul, of course, was a former Pharisee from Tarsus.

The church is called to be a sign of the kingdom, drawing people into the kingdom, where men and women 'from every nation, from all tribes and peoples and languages' will stand before the throne of God and the Lamb (Rev. 7:9). In a divided world the glory of a multicultural church is that already in the here and now it offers a window into the Kingdom of God that is to come.

EVANGELISM IS A PROCESS

When I was a child the classic way in which many became Christians was by responding to an appeal to come forward at the end of the sermon. It was a Damascus Road experience – a crisis when God broke into their lives.

I remember as a ten-year-old boy attending the Billy Graham Crusade at London's Harringay Arena in 1954 and watching hundreds, if not thousands, of people streaming forward to the front in response to the appeal. The Billy Graham Organisation claims it was the biggest evangelistic venture in the twentieth century – 1,750,000 people attended the meetings. In the 1950s, 1960s, and 1970s that was the kind of evangelism that worked.

Not surprisingly in my first church, which I pastored in 1973-1986, the style of evangelism emphasised the need for people to make a 'decision' for Christ. Within a matter of months of my arriving we supported an old-fashioned tent 'crusade' in Platt Fields, near the centre of Manchester. When Billy Graham came to Anfield, Liverpool in July 1984 we again organised coaches. In addition, along with inviting evangelists to come and run 'missions' in our church, we invited teams of students to come and help us engage in visitation evangelism ('cold calling') – the largest such team was in September 1977 when we had 37 students from Spurgeon's College leading a full-scale mission. As part of an American-inspired visitation scheme entitled 'Evangelism Explosion' we also trained up our own teams of evangelists who would fix appointments with church 'contacts' and within an hour or so of knocking on the door would seek to lead them to Christ – and it worked![1]

---

[1] This involved two diagnostic questions: 'Have you come to the place in your life where you know that if you died, you would go to heaven?' and 'If you were to stand before God and he were to ask you, "Why should I let you into my heaven?", what would you say?'

By the time I was minister of my second church (1993-2014) the world of evangelism had well and truly changed. It is reckoned that the last major successful evangelistic event in Britain was the Billy Graham Mission England crusade in 1984. After that people no longer responded to Billy Graham, or indeed to any other evangelist, in the way they once did. As a country we had changed. Whereas at one stage there were many lapsed Christians and many people on the fringes of the church, people who knew the basics of the faith and subscribed to them, things became very different. Today there is widespread ignorance about the Christian faith. There is no longer a harvest which evangelists can reap on a one-night stand. Instead evangelism is about sowing as well as reaping. Evangelism has become a process for which the local church now has to take responsibility: the day of the traditional travelling evangelist has gone.

As Bob Jackson put it, 'Evangelism has moved from being a call to repent from sin at the foot of the cross to travelling alongside those who are on a journey from lack of faith to Christian discipleship. Evangelism is no longer an event, it is a process.'[2] Instead of 'missions', we now have courses: Alpha, Believe, Christianity Explored and Discipleship Explored, Compass and Disciple, Emmaus, Just Looking, Pilgrim, and 'Y' to name but a few. People need time to become Christians. In Chelmsford we opted for Alpha – not because we necessarily thought it was the best course theologically, but because of its profile.[3] According to an Ipsos Mori survey conducted in the autumn of 2011, 25 per cent of British adults recognise Alpha. Even more significantly, according to an Ipsos Mori poll in 2010, 'nearly four million Britons, who have not done the course, expressed some degree of interest in it'. As a result, whenever we advertised an Alpha course on our church website or on a church poster, there were always takers. It was often the case that most of the people attending the Alpha course had no connection with our church.

---

[2] Bob Jackson, *Hope for the Church: Contemporary Strategies for Growth* (Church House, London, 2002), 80.
[3] I felt that just as there was a whole session devoted to the death of Christ, so too there should be a whole session devoted to the resurrection of Jesus and a whole session devoted to the person of Jesus. I was also uncomfortable with Alpha's teaching on healing, which seemed to give the impression that physical healing is the norm.

In many ways the development of process evangelism is very healthy. With people further and further away from the Christian faith, it is inevitable that the journey to faith takes longer. People need time to reflect on the Gospel and its demands before they commit themselves to Christ. Becoming a Christian is a massive step. It is a stepping from spiritual darkness into light. It is an act of life-long commitment. It radically affects the way we live our lives. It is only right and proper that people are not hurried. If the ordinary physical birth process takes nine months, then we should not be surprised if the spiritual birth process takes time too. I used to reckon the process normally took two years.

As I reflect on process evangelism, the following further thoughts come to mind:

- With the distance between the 'world' and the church ever increasing, courses like Alpha are not basic enough.[4] I am delighted to see that there are a number of 'pre-Alpha' courses developing. In this regard I commend *Well Springs*,[5] an innovative 'stepping stones' course designed by Leesa Barton (now McKay) to 'reach out to women who already have contact with Christians either through friendship, or church activities such as parent and child groups or keep fit classes'. It takes the form of a pampering course for women, dealing with issues such as rest and relaxation, acceptance and security, worry and anxiety, failure, beauty, healing and forgiveness, influences , and self-image. For instance, in the section on healing and forgiveness, Leesa creatively links the activity of doing a 'facial' (involving cleansing, toning and moisturising skin) with the basic

[4] Mark Ireland and Mike Booker, *Making New Disciples: Exploring the Paradoxes of Evangelism* (SPCK, London, 2015), 76, quotes the research of James Heard, who was on the staff of HTB for five years. Heard reported that of those attending the courses in his survey, 86 per cent were either already regular churchgoers or were from the 'open-dechurched' category; i.e. they had been baptised, had generally grown up with some church involvement, had left at some point and were open to the possibility of returning (*Inside Alpha*, Paternoster, 2009). As Ireland and Booker make clear, 'it does suggest that although Alpha is effective in evangelism, in the UK it predominantly draws from a fairly small – and shrinking – part of the population.' See also Andrew Brookes (ed.), *The Alpha Phenomenon: Theology Praxis and Challenges for Mission and Church Today* (Churches Together in Britain and Ireland, London, 2007).

[5] Leesa Barton, *Wellsprings: an eight-week course of refreshment and pampering looking at issues women face today, from a Christian perspective* (Baptist Union of Great Britain, Didcot, 2010).

need for everybody to be 'cleansed from the dirt and
grime of life'[6]). She also helped to develop a 'stepping
stones' course for seniors, entitled *Well Being*.

- There is a need for 'post-Alpha' type courses. For instance,
  I wrote a baptismal course entitled *Baptism, Belonging and
  Breaking of Bread.*[7] This course assumes that participants
  had already looked at such key discipleship themes as
  'Why and how do I pray?'; 'Why and how should I read the
  Bible?'; 'How does God guide us?'; 'How can I resist evil?';
  and 'Why and how should I tell others?'. Recognising
  that in the New Testament commitment to Christ always
  involved commitment to Christ's people, the course deals
  with baptism, the church, and the Lord's Supper.

- Recognising that with the increasing pressures of life
  'people need ever longer to get their heads around the faith
  and will commit ever shorter amounts of time',[8] instead of
  having introductory courses that last ten weeks or more,
  shorter 'bite-size' courses should be created. In this regard
  I note with interest the Pilgrim courses designed by the
  Church of England can be done in six weeks.

- Sometimes the contrast between the Damascus experience
  and the Emmaus experience is overdrawn. As Jonathan
  Roberts has argued, there is no reason why the journey
  to faith should not culminate in a decision made at an
  evangelistic service. For although most people's journey
  to faith is gradual, there are usually key moments in the
  process.[9] What is more, although the Christian life is a
  life-long journey, the reality is that there are significant
  stages on the way: commitment to Christ and his church
  in baptism would be one of those key stages.

---

[6] *Wellsprings*, 24.
[7] Paul Beasley-Murray, *Baptism, Belonging and Breaking Bread: Preparing for Baptism* (Baptist Union of Great Britain, Didcot, 2010).
[8] Bob Jackson quoted by Mark Ireland and Mike Booker, *Making New Disciples*, 89
[9] Jonathan Roberts, 'Inviting a response', *Ministry Today* 58 (Summer 2013) 28-29.

TRANSFER GROWTH IS A BONUS,
NOT A GOAL

When I arrived in my first church it was with one clear goal: to use 'all means' to win men and women for Jesus Christ (see 1 Cor. 9:22). Even before I had been inducted the church had circulated a letter around the neighbourhood which announced: 'Dr Beasley-Murray has now come to serve the community in Altrincham. He believes that Jesus Christ is the ultimate answer to man's need [sic – in those days 'man' was a generic term] and he is anxious that you too might come to know this'.

Almost immediately people came to faith and the church began to grow. In the first five years the membership of the church more than doubled. But I could see that the rate of growth we had been enjoying was beginning to slow down. For reasons for which I was unclear, we were not making the same impact that we had before. It was this concern that sparked off my initial interest in the American church growth movement. I read with interest *Your Church Can Grow* by Peter Wagner and was fascinated by his seven 'vital signs of a healthy growing church'[1]. As a result, I decided to test out his findings within a British context. With the help of my friend Alan Wilkinson, I ended up doing a massive survey of 350 English Baptist churches, which amassed more than 300,000 items of information. We eventually wrote up our findings in *Turning the Tide* in which we linked the survey with the church growth we were experiencing in Altrincham.[2]

---

[1] C. Peter Wagner, *Your Church Can Grow* (Regal, Glendale, 1976).

[2] Paul Beasley-Murray and Alan Wilkinson, *Turning the Tide:* In the preface Peter Wagner wrote: 'Paul Beasley-Murray has made such a striking contribution to church growth knowledge and literature through the publication of this book that it would be all too tempting to multiply superlatives like galaxies in the Milky Way. Never before has such a through empirical test been designed, an instrument applied, and the data processed by computer. This is the most objective, scientific study of church growth principles that I have seen.'

One of our key conclusions related to transfer growth: i.e. the movement of Christians from one church to another. Transfer growth can result from people moving homes; but it can also simply involve people moving churches within the same place. In the survey we became aware of churches whose growth had clearly been at the expense of another Baptist fellowship nearby. Transfer growth can be like Robin Hood in reverse: it robs the poor in order to give to the rich. In fact, from the perspective of the church left behind, such transfers are not growth, but loss. Although there can be a positive aspect to transfer growth – it can provide a major lifeline to what would otherwise be a seemingly hopeless situation – it can also be very destructive if it simply denudes other churches. Instead of encouraging transfer growth, we wanted to ensure that we focused on conversion growth: i.e. people with no church connections coming to repentance and faith and in turn then added to the church.[3]

In the light of the survey we developed a new model for church growth, where the emphasis was not on growing a church but on making and developing disciples.[4] We pictured the Great Commission of Matt. 28:18-19 in terms of a dynamic, spiral process. Obedience to the Great Commission involves winning people for Jesus Christ and developing them, so that they in turn may go out and win others, who will then go on to win others, and thereby repeat the process, with the church growing ever upwards.

On the basis of this spiral model, we identified four aspects of mission and ministry, through which people need to be moved 'round the spiral': serving and attracting (although two different activities – we do not serve in order to attract, we serve because need is there; however, there is often an attractive quality to our serving); winning men and women to Christ and his church; nurturing through building up people in their faith; and finally, preparing people for mission and ministry.

When church growth becomes the goal something has gone wrong somewhere. Alan Wilkinson, who at the time was the Administrator of the Manchester Business School, often used to quote a former chairman of McKinseys, a large U.S. management consultancy firm, who said that 'profit is not an end in itself but merely the reward of

---

[3] *Turning the Tide*, 54-56.
[4] *Turning the Tide*, 61-83.

good management'. In church terms, we might say 'growth is not an end in itself but merely the reward of good stewardship'. Of course, businesses need to make money, and of course churches need to grow. But just as a healthy business must not be dominated by making short-term profits, neither can a church – if it wants to remain healthy – be dominated by the numbers game. As Rick Warren has said in his writings on the purpose-driven church: 'I believe the key issues for churches in the 21st century will be church health, not church growth … Focussing on growth alone misses the point. When congregations are healthy, they grow the way God intends. Healthy churches don't need gimmicks to grow – they grow naturally.'[5]

Growth is healthy. Growth is a sign of life. Growth is what God intends for his church. But we need to distinguish between the various types of numerical growth: biological growth (children of Christian parents coming to faith and active membership); transfer growth, and conversion growth.[6] In particular, it is important to set the challenge to growth within the context of the Great Commission. The Risen Lord does not say 'Go and grow bigger and better churches', but rather 'Go and make disciples'. Growth may be the consequence of making disciples, but it is not the objective. It is important that we get our focus right.

In other words, transfer growth is always a bonus, and should not be a goal.

---

[5] Rick Warren, *The Purpose-Driven Church: Growth without Compromising Your Message and Mission* (Zondervan, Grand Rapids, 1995), 17.

[6] Numerical growth is not the only form of church growth. David Wasdell, an Anglican vicar then working in the East End of London, described a four-fold process of church growth based on Acts 2: (1) *Growing up* (Acts 2:42: 'They devoted themselves to the apostles' teaching and fellowship, to the breaking of bread and the prayers'): i.e. the deepening of individual understanding and enactment of the Christian faith, growth in Christian maturity. (2) *Growing together* (Acts 2:44: 'All who believed were together and had all things in common): i.e. the building of deep, loving interpersonal relationships which reflect the oneness which Christ shares with the Father. (3) *Growing out* (Acts 2:45: 'They would sell their possessions and distribute the proceeds to all, as any who had need'): i.e. the costly, loving, self-giving involvement of the church with all levels of society. (4) *Growing more* (Acts 2:47b: 'And day by day the Lord added to their number those who were being saved'): i.e. the adding of new Christians to the community of the Body of Christ.

THERE IS MORE TO MISSION THAN MAKING DISCIPLES

Unlike most minsters, I was ordained as a missionary rather than as a pastor. For within three days of my ordination Caroline and I together with our one-year-old son were on a ship bound for Congo, where I was due to teach New Testament and Greek in the Protestant Theological Faculty of the Free University of Congo. At the heart of my ordination vows was the Great Commission: 'Go and make disciples of all nations, baptising them in the name of the Father and of the Son and of the Holy Spirit, and teaching them to obey everything that I have commanded' (Matt. 28:19,20). For at the point of ordination I was asked:

> 'Acknowledging the supreme authority of our Lord and Saviour Jesus Christ, who has commissioned and commanded his Church to make disciples of all nations, do you freely receive his commission and do you promise to endeavour at all times to obey his command?'[1]

When we returned from our two-year stint in Africa and I became minister of Altrincham Baptist Church, the Great Commission still dominated all that I sought to do. In a statement that Alan Wilkinson and I drew up for the church, we said: that the mission of the church is:

- To bring men and women under the rule of Christ and into the committed membership of his church.
- To nurture new Christians and also those older in their

---

[1] Taken from the section on 'The commissioning of a missionary' in *Orders and Prayers for Church Worship: A Manual for Ministers* (Baptist Union, London, 4th edition, 1967), 229, compiled by Ernest Payne and Stephen Winward.

faith ... so that all may share their faith, win others for
Christ and his church and demonstrate by their words and
actions the love of God as shown in Jesus.[2]

Although we went on to say that one of the ways this is done
is 'by the acts of social service they perform, not only for the
fellowship but also in the community, both local and widespread',
the truth is that 'service' was secondary to 'the winning of people
to Christ and his Church'. At this stage in the 1970s our thinking
very much reflected the thinking of most British Evangelicals.

A sea-change began to take place in the thinking of Evangelicals
following the International Congress on World Evangelisation held
at Lausanne in 1974, from which the Lausanne Covenant came,
affirmed that 'evangelism and socio-political involvement are
both part of our Christian duty'.[3] True, 'in the church's mission of
sacrificial service evangelism is primary', but such evangelism, it
was recognised, must take place in the context of a 'deep and costly
penetration of the world'.[4] Slowly but surely, Evangelicals began
to wake up to the fact that evangelism and service are 'the two
blades of a pair of scissors or the two wings of a bird, and that just
as proclamation and service characterised the ministry of Jesus, so
they are to characterise ours'.[5]

Like many others I was deeply influenced by John Stott who
in his classic volume *Christian Mission in the Modern World*, argued
that the defining form of the Great Commission is not found in
Matt. 28:19-20 but rather John 20:21: 'As the Father sent me so
send I you.'[6] He went on to say that the Johannine form of the
Great Commission, according to which the church's mission is to
be modelled on the Son's, 'implies that we are sent into the world
to serve, and that the humble service we are to render will include
for us as it did for Christ both words and works, a concern for the
hunger and sickness of both body and soul'.[7]

---

[2] Paul Beasley-Murray and Alan Wilkinson, *Turning the Tide*, 66.
[3] The Lausanne Covenant, paragraph 5. See *For the Lord We Love: Study Guide to the Lausanne Covenant* (Lausanne Movement, 2nd edition, London, 2009).
[4] Lausanne Covenant, paragraph 6.
[5] *The Grand Rapids Report: Evangelism and Social Responsibility* (Paternoster, Carlisle, 1982), 23.
[6] See John Stott, Christian Mission in the Modern World, 1st edition, 1975; updated and expanded by Christopher Wright (IVP, London, 2015), 15-33.
[7] John Stott, *Christian Mission in the Modern World*, 28.

Later, in his report on the 1988 National Evangelical Anglican Celebration (NEAC 3) at Caister, Stott wrote: 'It is generally accepted amongst us that "mission" denotes everything Christ sends us into the world to do as his servants and witnesses. We are also clearer that 'compassionate service' cannot stop at philanthropy, but demands political action too in the quest for justice, for it is impossible to preach the gospel and ignore the social needs of those to whom we preach it.'[8]

As a result, when in 1993 I became minister of Central Baptist Church, Chelmsford, I introduced a new mission statement for the church, combining both the Matthean and Johannine forms of the Great Commission: 'Our mission is to go Christ's way and make disciples':

> On the one hand, 'to go Jesus way' is to model our mission on the mission of Jesus. Inevitably this means that our mission must be 'holistic', reflecting God's love and concern for every aspect of people's lives. Just as Jesus fed hungry mouths, washed dirty feet, and comforted the sad, so too must we. If our mission is to be patterned on the mission of Jesus, then our evangelism must always go hand in hand with costly compassionate service.
>
> On the other hand, 'to make disciples' means that our mission includes winning people to Christ and to his church. However, our evangelism goes far beyond calling men and women to decide for Christ. Discipleship is in view. As Jesus himself made clear (e.g. Mark 8:34) discipleship is costly and involves an ongoing commitment to follow Jesus. Inevitably this means going against the stream of world opinion – it means making Jesus Lord of every area of our lives.

As a church we committed ourselves to a 'holistic' form of mission: on the one hand we developed an evangelistic strategy at the heart of which were our Alpha courses; on the other hand we ran clubs for people with mental health difficulties, a child contact centre for broken families, budget coaching services for people

---

[8] John Stott, *What is the Spirit Saying?* (Church of England Evangelical Council, Chippenham, 1988), 6.

having difficulty managing their finances and a community resource centre for disadvantaged Africans moving into Chelmsford.

Now in my retirement I worship at Chelmsford Cathedral, where the words 'As the Father sent me, so send I you' have become the foundation of all that the Cathedral seeks to do. This means that first and foremost the Cathedral is there for others – it is a 'sent' community. In the words of Nicholas Henshall, the Dean of the Cathedral, 'Jesus makes it absolutely clear that ministry to the marginalised, the broken and the lost is the first priority of the Christian community, not an added extra. It is the major theme of Jesus first sermon in Luke 4:16-21 and his last piece of discipleship training in Matthew 25:31-46'.[9] But this is not to exclude our obligation to share the good news with others: hence the appointment of a new full-time member of the clergy team with responsibility for evangelism and discipleship.

Winning people to Jesus Christ and his church is vital: in that respect I identify fully with the Apostle Paul when he declared 'Woe to me if I preach not the Gospel' (1 Cor. 9:16); as also when he wrote 'We are ambassadors for Christ, since God is making his appeal through us; we entreat you on behalf of Christ, be reconciled to God' (2 Cor. 5:20). However, there is more to mission than making disciples: we have a world to serve as well as to win.

[9] Michael and Nicholas Henshall, *Dear Nicholas* (Sacristy Press, Durham, 2019), 68.

THE KINGDOM IS NOT THE CHURCH

I have often said, 'The local church is the cutting edge of the kingdom.' For me there is no higher calling than to be a minister of a local church.[1] However, I have come to realise that the kingdom of God is far bigger than the local church: there is a bigger world beyond the church where God wants his people to live and serve.[2]

Unfortunately, many ministers are often so focussed on their church that they do not see the bigger picture. Consequently, they suck all the time and energy of their people into the church, instead of sending them out to serve God in the world. For them 'every member ministry' is above all about using gifts and talents in the church rather than the world.

Yet for Jesus discipleship is about being salt and light in the world (Matt. 5:13-16). Mission begins on a Monday! It is in the world where Christians are called to live out their discipleship and to claim the world for Jesus. When the first Christians proclaimed 'Jesus is Lord', they were not in the first place saying 'Jesus is my Lord', nor even 'Jesus is Lord of the church', but 'Jesus is the Lord of the world' (see Phil. 2:9-11; Col. 1:15-20). Christians, if they are to be true to their faith, must not retreat into ecclesiastical ghettoes, but take their stand in the world, which is the Lord's. In the words of a World Council of Churches document, 'The real battles of faith today are being fought in factories, shops, offices and farms, in political parties and government agencies, in countless homes, in press, radio and television, in the relationship of nations.'[3]

---

[1] See Paul Beasley-Murray, *This Is My Story: A Story Of Life, Faith and Ministry* (Wipf and Stock, Eugene, Oregon, 2018), 10.
[2] See, for instance, Peter Wagner, *Your Church Can Grow*, 69-83, where the 'mobilisation of the laity' refers only to people using their gifts in the local church.
[3] Mark Greene, *The Great Divide* (London Institute for Contemporary Christianity, 2010), 20.

Christian ministry and mission are not about what Christians
do with their spare time, but what about they do with the whole
of life. According to Neil Hudson of the London Institute for
Contemporary Christianity, in any given week a maximum of ten
hours may be given to church activities, with a further 48 hours
given to sleeping, which then leaves 110 hours per week for work,
family and leisure: 'this 110-hour space is our primary arena for
mission and discipleship'. In the light of this Hudson asked: 'How
can we best use the ten hours that we spend together to equip one
another to live well for Christ in the other 110?'[4]

The kingdom is bigger than the church. The Australian John
Mallison perceptively commented: 'Never overlook the fact that
some will be called to a place of service in the community, in
local government, civic leadership or a trade union, and never feel
called to work in the programmes of the church. The church needs
to affirm and support those with this call. Our task is not to pull all
the godly out of the world and put them to work for the church.'[5]

Ministers also need to help their people see that whatever job
they may do can be a ministry. Unfortunately, the church has
tended to see only certain jobs as true 'vocations'. As Mark Greene
said with tongue in cheek: 'SSD [the 'Sacred-Secular Divide']
leads us to believe that really holy people become missionaries,
moderately holy people become pastors, and people who are not
much use to God get a job.' He went on: 'Beyond that, SSD teaches
us that there is a hierarchy of holiness even among the 98 percent
of non-church-paid Christians. SSD teaches us that people involved
in the caring professions – nurses, social workers, teachers – are
holier than those involved in industry or commerce. Indeed, it's
because of SSD that the church has historically treated business
with some distaste, failing to recognise that the poor need jobs, not
just aid, and that there is poverty without wealth generation. As
one businessman put it: 'The church appreciates my tithe but not
the enterprise that gives rise to it'.'[6]

A creative way of helping people discover that their work can be
a form of Christian ministry was given by Richard Broholm, who

---

[4] Neil Hudson, *Imagine Church: Releasing Whole-Life Disciples* (IVP, Nottingham, 2012).
[5] John Mallison, *Grid* (Summer 1987).
[6] Mark Greene, *The Great Divide*, 11.

looked at what people do in relationship to the threefold office of Christ's ministry as 'priest', 'prophet', and 'king'. In terms of the priestly or pastoral ministry of Christ's body, he wrote: 'What we have often failed to see is that the contractor who builds houses, the lab technician who tests for cancer, and the postal worker who bridges the gap between other distant friends are all engaged in a caring ministry even though it is unlikely they will ever intimately know the persons they serve'.[7]

Over the years I regularly interviewed within the context of public worship not just people involved in community service such as social workers, teachers, policemen, prison officers, health visitors, doctors and nurses; but also those working in the 'rag trade' and in banking, on building sites and in call centres, managing shops and overseeing 'diversity' programmes in a large business. I asked four questions:

- What will you be doing this time tomorrow?
- How does your faith influence your work?
- What opportunities do you have to share your faith?
- How can the church best pray for you?

Although the focus was on the individual, as the congregation listened to the interview, they also began to reflect on their own work and how their faith impacted upon their work.

The church's small groups can also be encouraged to relate the world of work to their Christian faith. For example, a group might decide to put aside its traditional pattern of Bible study, and instead of starting with a Bible passage begin with where people are.

It is in the world where the real battles of faith take place. Yet in the words of Hans Ruedi-Weber,

> In churches all over the world ... the majority of those who have made the *sacramentum* [baptismal vows] do not actually join Christ's struggle for the world. After taking 'the military oath', many of them become deserters, conforming themselves to the world, and not being transformed by the

---

[7] Richard Broholm, 'Towards Claiming and Identifying our Ministry in the Work Place' in George Peck and John Hoffmann (eds.), *The Laity in Ministry* (Judson, Valley Forge, Pennsylvania, 1984).

renewal of their minds (Rom. 12:2). Others go on permanent leave, only returning occasionally for a military inspection. They lead a double life, following two different sets of ethics – one for their private, Sunday life, and one for their life in the workaday world. Still others always remain recruits in the barracks, becoming more and more refined in the use of the spiritual armour of God, but never leaving their Christian camp in order to fight for reconciliation for the world. Under these circumstances, no wonder the battle soon begins in the barracks![8]

The kingdom is bigger than the church. The saints need to be equipped to fulfil 'their ministry' (Eph. 4:12) in the wider world!

---

[8] Hans Ruedi Weber, *Salty Christians* (Seabury Press, New York, 1963), 26.

THE KEY TO PASTORING IS LOVING

I sometimes wonder whether the Risen Lord might just as well have said to Peter 'love' my sheep instead of 'care for' my sheep. For I have discovered that that the key to effective pastoring is loving. Indeed, the key to effective church leadership, is loving – for people will only follow where they feel loved and cared for.

Or to restate this is in another way: effective Christian leadership can never just be task-orientated, it must also be people-orientated too. Within a voluntary organisation such as a church, the mission of the church can only be achieved if people feel valued for themselves, and not just for the work they may achieve. It is only as people sense that they are loved and cared for that they will cooperate in seeking to follow the lead that is being set.

One sign that leaders care for people is that they know their people. They know them by name. They know their individual circumstances and their individual concerns. Just as Jesus the Good Shepherd knew his sheep and was willing to lay down his life for his sheep (John 10:14, 15), so ministers in their role as 'pastors' need to know those entrusted to their care and to be willing to give of themselves to their care. Without such expressions of tangible love and care, people may well be reluctant to support their minister's initiatives. In this regard I find the Apostle Paul's final instructions in 1 Cor: 16 instructive: 'Now brothers and sisters, you know that members of the household of Stephanas … have devoted themselves to the service (*diakonia*) of the saints. I urge you to put yourselves at the service of such people' (1 Corinthians 16:15,16). It would appear that Stephanas and his extended family were already exercising leadership within the church, but Paul here urges the church not to 'follow their leadership' (GNB) because of the position they held, but because of the way in which they had given of themselves in the service of God's people.

As I look back on the thirteen years of my ministry in my first church in Altrincham, I was blessed with a church which willingly followed the lead I gave. There must have been times when my people questioned my leadership: for instance I remember how on one Pentecost Sunday evening, without having given any notice to anyone, I told the congregation that there would be no service, instead we would all go 'cold-calling', (i.e. going from door to door) and seek to share the good news of Jesus. Nobody dissented. Did it help, I wonder, that every day I was in the homes of my people?

By contrast, the opening years of my ministry in Chelmsford were tough. The vast majority of the church happily responded to my leadership – but a handful (and it only takes a handful) decided to oppose me at every twist and turn. This was the context in which I wrote the following 'confession of practice':

> The key to my ministry is the love I exude to others. If my ministry is not constantly permeated by a warm, generous, and affirming spirit, then I may as well give up.
>
> It doesn't matter how dedicated I am in the spiritual disciplines, how hard I work at my sermons, how carefully I prepare my prayers for public worship, if I'm not in love with my people then all my pious words won't make a whit of difference. The only effective sounding board for the Gospel is love.
>
> Likewise, so long as people don't feel I love them, all my professional expertise is of no avail: my grasp of church growth principles, my counselling skills, my visionary leadership, will get the church nowhere. It is love that enthuses, love that inspires, love that motivates.
>
> The fact is that my ministry will be successful to the degree that I love those in my care. Without such love, then all the sacrifices I have made as a minister will be in vain – my willingness to take a drop in stipend, my working all the hours God gives, will, of themselves, benefit nobody.

What does all this mean in practice? It means

- Being patient with the awkward squad, even when they seem to be deliberately obtuse;
- Having time for everybody, even for those who criticise me behind my back;
- Keeping quiet about my achievements, allowing others to boast about theirs – or about their kids;
- Respecting those less able than myself – after all, they are doubtless better at plugging a wall than I am;
- Treating everybody with old-fashioned courtesy, never riding roughshod over the feelings of others.

Yes, loving the church will mean not standing on my dignity, forcing the church to go 'my way' but rather giving people space to make their decisions before God. It means never allowing others to cause me to lose my 'cool'. If people fail to respond to my leadership, then perhaps this means I've not been loving them enough (or, of course, I may have been wrong!).

Because each individual in the fellowship is of value to me, I will not stand for any gossip – nor will I indulge in title-tattle myself. Rather I will always seek to be positive and praise the achievements of others, whether they be great or small.

When things get tough for individuals, I'll be there, standing by them; I'll always believe the best of another, even if they've let me down in the past; I'll never give up hope in anybody; I'll put up with misrepresentation rather than allow the church to suffer.

From beginning to end I'll seek to ensure that love is the chief characteristic of my ministry. One day preaching and praying will come to an end; but there will be no end to loving. My preaching and praying are only touching aspects of the truth; but my loving is the way of truth. Clearly faith and hope are vital to any minister, but love is the great essential pre-requisite for any ministry.'

Thankfully, those first seven challenging years gave way to a further fourteen very happy years. Love, not confrontation, finally triumphed. Yes, the key to pastoring is loving.

PASTORAL VISITING HAS NOT HAD ITS DAY

In times past, one of the chief tasks of the minister was to visit people in their homes. Some still do, many do not. Nolan Harmon told of one energetic Baptist minister who used to get into every home in his church – he had over 2000 members – once every year. His calls were necessarily short, about ten minutes each, nonetheless he got them made.[1] But Harmon was writing in 1928. In 1996 I undertook a survey of some 141 ministers of mainline Protestant churches: on average they claimed to spend 7.5 hours a week in pastoral visiting.[2] My impression is that things are very different now. Although there are still some ministers who make pastoral visiting a major part of their ministry, others set aside just an afternoon a week, while some seem to have given up altogether on visiting, and instead prefer to keep in touch by phone or by email. They expect people to come and see them in their office, rather for them to go and see people in their homes.

Some guides to pastoral care now question the value of pastoral visiting. Eugene Peterson, for instance, suggested that routine pastoral visiting had little point.

> I want to be a pastor who listens. I want to have the energy and time to really listen to them so when they are through, they know at least one other person has some inkling of what they're feeling and thinking ... Too much of pastoral visitation is punching the clock, assuring people we're on the job, being busy, earning our pay.'[3]

---

[1] Nolan B. Harmon, *Ministerial Ethics and Etiquette* (Abingdon, Nashville, revised edition, 1978), 83.
[2] Paul Beasley-Murray, *Power for God's Sake: Power and Abuse in the Local Church* (Paternoster, Carlisle, 1998) 48.
3 Eugene Peterson, 'The Unbusy Pastor', *Leadership* II (Summer 1981), 72.

Similarly, Stephen Pattison has argued against routine pastoral visiting on the grounds that it accomplishes very little, because there is no agreed understanding why a visit is taking place. Often the minister has no clear purpose, and even if the minister does have a motive for visiting, this motive is not normally communicated to the person visited. Add to that the residual 'judgmental aspect' of the ministerial role, and you end up with not only a pointless visit, but possibly an unwelcome visit too.[4]

Much depends on the skill of a minister. Ministers with 'knowledge and understanding' (Jer. 3:15) can certainly engage in conversations which get below the surface. This was my experience. Like the Apostle Paul at Ephesus (Acts 20:20), every visit I made had purpose. Even ministers in larger churches should still be engaged in pastoral visiting. To quote Pope Francis:

> The priest who doesn't go out of himself, who mixes little with people, loses the best part of the people, the part that is able to activate the deepest part of our priestly heart. He who doesn't get out of himself, instead of becoming a mediator, gradually becomes an intermediary, a manager... That is the explanation for the dissatisfaction of some who end up being sad and transformed, as it were, into collectors of antiques or novelties, instead of being shepherds smelling of sheep, shepherds in the middle of their own flock, and fishers of men ... I ask you: be shepherds smelling of sheep, they must be smelled'![5]

Pastoral visiting enables ministers to get to know their people. I believe ministers should have visited their people at least once in their home: for only in that way can a pastoral relationship be truly established. It is in their home that a person generally risks being real. It is difficult putting up a façade. Even without anything so much as being said, the discerning minister can begin to understand the context from which a person comes. There is no better way of getting to know a person than visiting them in their home. There is therefore a lot to be said for ministers within the first year or

---

[4] Stephen Pattison, *A Critique of Pastoral Care*, 75, 76.
[5] Quoted by Elisabeth Pique in *Pope Francis: Life and Revolution, a biography of Jorge Bergoglio* (Darton, Longman and Todd, London, 2015), 190.

so of their call to a church aiming to visit all the members in their homes. Some ministers beginning their ministry in a new church feel it is more effective arranging for people to visit them in their church office, but while such a method may be more effective in the use of time, in the long run it proves less effective in getting to know and understand those in their charge.

Pastoral visits are needed to visit people who are new to the church. In a large church, where every Sunday there are 'newcomers' this can be quite demanding – but it is also very rewarding. I confess that I was often direct in such visits; so much so that I often began the conversation by apologising for the fact that I would be somewhat like the Gestapo in the questions I asked. But then, that seems to me to be the task of a minister. A minister is not a counsellor, who just listens and responds: a minister can probe and even challenge. If, for instance, I was visiting a couple who were living together, I would, in a gentle way, make it clear that I did not approve of their living arrangements and would tell them that I would be delighted to regularise their situation. It was amazing how many weddings eventually then took place! I asked people to tell me where they were born and brought up and got them to go through their past. I got them to share with me their faith journey. Only then did I begin to talk about our church, what it does in our community, how it functions, and what it might have to offer them. So much depended on the individual, as to how the conversation then proceeded. For me visiting newcomers was a vital pastoral task, as important as leading the church and expounding God's Word.

Then there is 'crisis' visiting. The 'crisis' may involve sadness or tragedy – the diagnosis of a terminal illness or the death of a loved one; or it may involve joy and celebration such as a birth or a wedding. Although I happily delegated routine visiting, I found it a great privilege to be there as people went through the lifecycle of birth, marriage and death. Others could share in the visiting where people might be in hospital for a week more, but I made it my priority to go and pray with hospitalised members at least once during their stay.

Every visit needs to be sacramental. In visiting the housebound this may involve bread and wine - I loved taking communion to the 'shut-ins' in the week leading up to Christmas and to Easter. But more generally I sought to make every visit 'sacramental' in the sense that it became 'a means of grace'. This means at the very least ending every visit with prayer. In many a home I would also read the Scriptures (often one of the lectionary readings for the day). This I believe is all part and parcel of being a minister.

Finally, how much visiting should a minister do? So much depends on the context. The only yardstick I have come across is Kennon Callahan's principle of visitation: 'Spend one hour in pastoral visitation each week for every minute you preach on a Sunday morning'.[6] Goodness, if some ministers were to adopt that principle, their sermons would become considerably shorter!

---

[6] Kennon L. Callahan, *Twelve Keys to an Effective Church* (Harper, San Francisco, 1983), 12.

PASTORAL CARE REQUIRES ORGANISATION

Pastoral care is one of the great privileges of ministry. Nobody else has the entry that ministers do into people's homes. No other person can draw alongside people in their joys and in their sorrows as a pastor. Paul Cedar, writing for ministers, rightly said: 'We give up an essential ministry when we give up pastoral care. Pastoral care is not only one of the greatest needs of our fast-growing impersonal society, it is also a unique privilege of the pastor.'[1]

However, although ministers may have the ultimate responsibility for pastoral oversight, the task of pastoral care is to be shared with others. For first and foremost pastoral care is just an expression of 'the new commandment' Jesus gave to his disciples to love one another (John 13:34). As Stephen Pattison put it, 'pastoral care is, in essence, surprisingly simple. It has one fundamental aim: to help people to know love, both as something to be received and something to give'.[2]

We see this emphasis on mutual care in the writings of the Apostle Paul. Likening the church to a body, he spoke of members having 'the same care for one another' (1 Cor. 12:25). He urged the Galatians to 'bear one another's burdens', which in turn involved caring for those straying from the faith and restoring the backsliders (Gal. 6:1, 2). Within the context of death and bereavement the Thessalonians were told to 'encourage one another and build one another up' (1 Thess. 5:11). Indeed, Paul expected the Thessalonians to share in every aspect of pastoral care: 'admonish the idlers, encourage the faint-hearted, help the

---

[1] Paul Cedar, 'The unique role of the pastor', 18 in P. Cedar, K Hughes and B. Patterson, *Mastering the Pastoral Role* (Multnomah, Portland, 1991).

[2] Alastair Campbell, *Paid To Care? The Limits of Professionalism in Pastoral Care* (SPCK, London, 1985), 1.

weak' (1 Thess. 5:14). Similarly, the Colossians were to 'teach and admonish one another in all wisdom' (Col. 3:16). Pastoral care was not exclusive to a particular cadre in the church: all were involved in 'the work of ministry' (see Eph. 4:12, 15, 16).[3]

To be most effective, pastoral care requires organisation. This means that in the first place, ministers must be organised themselves. Visiting 'on a whim' tends to be a waste of time. There needs to be a plan and a purpose. Appointments need to be the norm – otherwise people may be out or it may just be inconvenient. Furthermore, there is a lot to be said for notes to be made of the conversations held (whether in the home, the minister's office, a coffee shop or wherever). When I began as a young minister I tended to store information in my memory alone; however, I quickly realised the value of writing up the conversation on my return home or later the next day. It helps too keeping a record of significant dates such as baptisms, weddings, deaths – what a difference it can make when a minister sends a card or makes a visit on the first anniversary of a death! Ministers, if they are to care effectively for their people, need to be well-organised themselves.

Even in the smallest of churches ministers need to share the work of pastoral care. They need to encourage everybody in the church to care for one another. How that works out will depend upon the size of the church and the way in which the church is structured. My own conviction is that small groups are an effective way of sharing pastoral care in any church. For small groups are not just about Bible study and discussion. Rather, as I wrote recently in a flyer promoting small groups:

- Fellowship groups are about friendship, community, and sharing life together. They are places where people can relax with one another, laugh with one another, and even weep with one another: they are about being real with one another.

- Fellowship groups are about caring for one another, being there for one another, praying for one another, and offering practical support for one another.

---

3 See Paul Beasley-Murray, 'Paul as Pastor' in G.F. Hawthorne and R.P. Martin (eds.), *Dictionary of Paul and his Letters* (IVP, Leicester, 1993).

- Fellowship groups are about reading the Bible together and discovering how God's Word applies to our everyday lives.
- Fellowship groups are about encouraging one another to share the good news of Jesus with others.

However, small groups cannot care for everybody. Not everybody can be part of a small group: parents with young families, commuters working long hours, and 'professionals' who need to bring work back home every evening, may well not have the time to attend; while others, such as the elderly, may just not be able to get out to a small group.

In many churches the organisations and activity groups of a church provide pastoral care. 'Sunday School' teachers or youth group leaders can be very good in caring for those in their charge. The same is often true of leaders of all the other activities and organisations a church may run. But there are always some who get missed. Furthermore, not everybody belongs to a church organisation or activity group.

Churches need to find a way of caring for everybody in one way or another associated with them. This requires further organisation. In both my churches I found it helpful to set up a small pastoral team, which normally met every six weeks and was responsible for overseeing the pastoral care of the church. In the words of a job specification I produced:

> In the first place, this involves ensuring that the members and friends of the church are cared for, recognising that pastoral care involves not just helping the hurting, but also encouraging people to grow and develop in their Christian faith. Pastoral care also ensures caring for the well-being of the church as a whole, which in turn involves helping individual members and friends to feel part of the church and its mission.

Although I belonged to the pastoral team, I never wanted to be its team leader – rather I made myself accountable to the team. In this way we became accountable to one another in how we fulfilled our pastoral calling. True, there were limits to pastoral confidences which can be shared, but there is always a lot of information which can be mentioned, and which in turn enables the team as a whole to become more effective in its caring.

In many churches a small pastoral team might be sufficient. However, in larger churches it can be helpful to have additional pastoral 'helpers' responsible for designated families or individuals. As I wrote in a briefing note for such 'helpers':

> In a church as large as ours it is very easy for people to feel lost and uncared for. Your primary task is to ensure that all those in your care feel loved, wanted and cared for – in a sense you represent the Lord and his love to them. To keep track of people in your care, you may find it helpful to have an informal 'register', in which you mark absences from church! A secondary role is to be the eyes and ears of the ministers and the pastoral team. Please inform us of concerns: e.g. sickness, loneliness, loss of faith, family problems, redundancy, etc.

None of this is 'rocket-science'. It is relatively easy organising pastoral care in a church. However, none of this will work without ministers empowering, inspiring, and encouraging people to share in this vital ministry.

EVERYONE IS WOUNDED

Life is tough and none of us escapes unscathed. In differing ways all of us end up being wounded. I find it fascinating that Leonard Cohen in his song *First We Take Manhattan* expressed the same idea, for there he has the line: 'Well, it's Father's Day, and everybody's wounded'. Precisely what Cohen had in mind I do not know. Was he referring to his experience of being a son or to his experience of being the father of two children? For many family life can be extraordinarily painful – not least when parents reject their children and children reject their parents.

Family life can become a war zone. For instance, on average the police in England and Wales receive over 100 calls relating to domestic abuse every hour. But these calls do not tell the whole story. According to the 2018 Crime Survey of England and Wales only 18 per cent of women who had experienced partner abuse in the previous 12 months had reported the abuse to the police. That same survey estimated that 28.9 per cent (4.8 million) of women aged 16-59 have experienced some form of domestic abuse since the age of 16 years. Then there is child abuse: here figures are uncertain but research with 2,275 young people aged 11-17 suggested that around 1 in 20 children in the UK have been sexually abused.

Marriage today is becoming a minority option in the UK. Of those who do marry, 60 per cent of their marriages are expected to end within twenty years. Think of all the broken dreams that this statistic represents.

The pain of life is seen in the increasing number of young people self-harming. In 2014 figures were published suggesting a 70 per cent increase in 10-14-year olds attending Accident & Emergency for self-harm related reasons over the preceding two years. It is thought that around 13 per cent of young people aged between 11 and 16 have self-harmed, although the actual figure could be much higher.

In 2018 there were 6,507 suicides – this represents a rate of 11.2 deaths per 100,000 population. Men aged 45 to 49 years had the highest age-specific suicide rate (27.1 deaths per 100,000 males).

In 2018 more than 70 million prescriptions for antidepressants were dispensed in England – this was almost double the 36 million dispensed a decade ago in 2008. People are finding it difficult to cope with life.

However, these and other such statistics do not tell the whole story about the pain people experience. People are wounded in a thousand and one different ways, at home, at work and in the community. To name but a few of the 'woundings', friendships break up, a loved one dies, promotion is denied, a job is lost, health breaks down, an investment fails. In one way or another, hopes are dashed or life becomes unfair. For some the scars are visible, but for many those scars are concealed.

Furthermore, church people are just as wounded as anybody else. Behind the apparently happy and contented faces of the Sunday morning congregation there is much pain that people do not dare to reveal. In one way or another everybody is wounded. If we are honest with ourselves, all of us need healing.

Where can that healing come from? For many the wounds are so deep and traumatic that specialist long-term counselling is required. In many instances time alone does not heal: the pain needs to be faced and the anger needs to be expressed before any moving on can begin. I know from my own personal experience how helpful this kind of therapy can be. Indeed, were the resources available, I think that everybody could benefit from becoming truly self-aware so that they can deal with the disappointments, pain, and hurt of life. However, the reality is that for less severe wounds the pastoral care of the church may prove to be sufficient for healing to take place. Here I have in mind not just the care offered by a skilful minister, but also the care of a home group where love and support can be received.

Yet we should not forget that for Christians the ultimate healer is Christ himself. He is the 'wounded healer' par excellence. He knows what it is to be hurt and wounded and even destroyed – and yet to overcome. It is the crucified and risen Christ who alone gives us the strength to live and to move on beyond the pain. Where do we encounter this crucified and risen Christ? Surely supremely as we gather around his Table. It is there as we eat bread and drink wine that healing may be found. In this regard I have discovered that the words used at communion within both the Roman Catholic and Anglican tradition are helpful. Just before the bread and wine are given the 'President' says:

> *Jesus is the Lamb of God who takes away the sin of the world.*
> *Blessed are those who are called to his supper.*

The people reply:

> *Lord, I am not worthy to receive you,*
> *but only say the word and I will be healed.*

It is the people's response which is significant. In a form of words reminiscent of the centurion's appeal to Jesus to heal his servant (see Matt. 8:8: 'Lord I am not worthy to have you come under my roof; but only speak the word and my servant shall be healed'), we look expectantly to Christ to carry on his work of healing in our lives. For whenever we eat bread and drink wine, we open our lives afresh to him and experience again his healing power. As Michael Sean Winters commented: 'In our deepest, darkest, most broken selves, the parts where we do not want to let the light shine, where we prefer not even to consider because it just hurts too much, Jesus can shine His light and bring healing'.[1]

---

[1] Michael Sean Winters, *Distinctly Catholic* blog, 22 August 2013.

PEOPLE NEED TO BE AFFIRMED – CONSTANTLY

In my early ministry I had two short exchange pastorates in the USA: the first at Buffalo Lick Baptist Church in Kentucky, the second at Peach Tree Baptist Church in Atlanta, Georgia. There I experienced affirmation 'in overdrive'. At the end of every service people would come up to me at the church door and tell me 'what a mighty fine preacher' I was. One Sunday evening I had had enough, so instead of going to the door to say goodbye to people, I just stood by the pulpit. To my embarrassment, people lined up at the pulpit to tell me what a 'mighty fine preacher' I was. It all seemed too unreal.

Still at least those expressions of praise were better than a gift I once received at a staff Christmas lunch, where 'Secret Santa' gave me a collection of 365 'pick-me-ups' to help me have 'a really great day'. So, on January 1st, I decided to give this 'Compliment A Day' a try. It proved impossible:

Day 1:   'You are on top of things.'
Day 2:   'You are so in control of things today – it's uncanny.'
Day 3:   'You'd better know how to take a compliment because the way you look today they're going to come thick and fast.'
Day 4:   'You're just brimming with confidence today.'
Day 5:   'Today – only the sky's the limit.'
Day 6:   'You are just the bee's knees.'
Day 7:   'Damn – you look like sex on legs!'

I quickly gave up on this pad of 'pick me ups'. It was all too pseudo – and of, course, untrue. There is a place for affirmation, but not for make-believe and self-adulation.

By contrast with our distant American 'cousins', who major on positivity, we Brits – together with our nearer Australian and New Zealander cousins – tend to be critical of the achievements of others. One expression of this critical approach to others is the so-called 'tall poppy syndrome', in which we put down other people who in one way or another have done well. We, as it were, cut down the tallest poppies in the field so that they are the same size of others. But that is often untrue and unfair, and born out of envy. By contrast Margaret Thatcher, prior to becoming Prime Minister, explained her political philosophy to an American audience as 'let your poppies grow tall'.[1] That is a much more positive approach to life. Although, on reflection, perhaps we should not just talk about letting our poppies grow tall: in view of the diversity of people's gifts, maybe we should recognise that not just the poppies, but the roses and tulips and other beautiful flowers too. Whatever, we need to affirm the talents and achievements of others.

I shall never forget my first experience of Spring Harvest, the Easter holiday Bible teaching event, where I had been invited to be one of the main speakers. On the first full day there was a meeting of speakers and helpers at which one of the leaders challenged us to major on the positive. Instead of being critical about the sessions, he asked us to find something positive to say about one another. Amazingly, this was what happened. By the end of the week I seemed to be walking on air. It was a wonderfully affirming experience.

Precisely because affirmation makes such a difference, when I later came to draw up a team covenant for my staff, one of the practices I encouraged was positivity. 'In our relationships with one another – and indeed with the rest of the church – we will always exude a positive spirit. We will shun negative talking and thinking. We will instead affirm one another and will speak well of one another.'

I had learnt that if we want to get the best from people, then appreciation is what is required. According to William James, 'The

---

[1] Margaret Thatcher, Speech to Pilgrims of the United States, Union Club, New York, 19 September 1975.

deepest principle in human nature is the craving to be appreciated'.[2] We all have our ups and downs. What a difference a word of encouragement then makes. I am reminded of a legend, which told of how one day God decided to reduce the weapons in the Devil's armoury. God told Satan that he could choose only one 'fiery dart'. Satan chose the power of discouragement, on the ground that 'if only I can persuade Christians to be thoroughly discouraged, they will make no further effort and I shall be enthroned in their lives'. Although but a legend, it does point to the desirability of regular encouragement. Indeed, this is what Scripture affirms (see 1 Thess. 5:11 & Heb.. 10:25).

It is also what the psychologists affirm. In a ground-breaking paper entitled 'The theory of human motivation' Abraham Maslow argued that esteem is one of five basic human needs: He wrote: 'All people in our society (with a few pathological exceptions) have a need or desire for a stable, firmly based, (usually) high evaluation of themselves, for self-respect, or self-esteem, and for the esteem of others. By firmly based self-esteem, we mean that which is soundly based upon real capacity, achievement and respect from others. Satisfaction of the self-esteem need leads to feelings of self-confidence, worth, strength, capability and adequacy of being useful and necessary in the world'.[3]

In other words, if we are to motivate volunteers, then we need to affirm this. In this regard it is not enough to write a thank-you note to people who helped at a church event – good leaders will also say how much they appreciated the help that was given and what a difference that help has made. Even better, good leaders will express their appreciation publicly. What a difference it makes when ministers publicly praise members of their congregation for their achievements, rather than themselves take the credit for what has happened. This ensures that in a church there is always a large base of willing volunteers.

Now as a retired minister, on a Sunday I look for what was good in the sermon and to express my appreciation accordingly. I find it significant that the Greek verb which is normally translated by

[2] William James, 'Letter to his class of Radcliffe College, 6 April 1898' in *Letters, Vol 2* (Longmans, Green & Co, 1920), 23.
[3] Abraham Maslow, *Motivation and Personality* (Harper, New York, 1954).

our English word 'encourage' (*parakaleo*) literally means to 'come alongside'. It can have the sense of to 'instil someone with courage or cheer', and the cognate noun ('Paraclete') is used by John of the Holy Spirit in Jesus' farewell discourses (John 14-16). I like to think that when I draw alongside a minister with a word of affirmation and encouragement, I am sharing in the ministry of God himself. The fact is that constant affirmation, which is rooted in reality, builds up others.

SENIORS ALSO WANT TO GROW

As a young minister in my twenties I thought that anybody over the age of 40 was old. From the perspective of ancient society, I was right. The Romans called a man under 40 a *iuvenis*, i.e. a young man ('juvenile'); while a man over 40 was called a *senex*, i.e. an old man ('senile'). In the ancient world there was no such thing as middle age.

Today, however, with more and more people surviving into their late 80s and beyond, defining old age gets increasingly difficult. Paul Stevens adopted three sub-categories for old age: 'young olds' are 60-69; 'old olds' are 70-79; and 'oldest olds' are 80 plus.[1] The World Health Organisation, recognising that the term 'old' is insufficient, suggested that 'the elderly' are 60-74 years of age, whilst 'the aged' are 75 years and above.

Frankly as a senior I find these categories demeaning. Although my energy levels are not the same as when I was 21, nonetheless at the age of 76 I don't feel an 'old old'; I certainly don't feel 'elderly', nor am I 'aged'. I therefore read with great interest the suggestion of Camilla Cavendish that old age for most people does not begin until they hit 74 – up until 74 people are 'middle-aged'.[2]

Not surprisingly, therefore many older people don't really feel old. In a survey of people over 80 conducted over thirty years ago, although 53 per cent admitted they were old, 36 per cent reported that they considered themselves middle-aged and 11 per cent young.[3] According to American research anthropologist, Sharon Kaufmann, 'When old people talk about themselves, they express a sense of self that's ageless – an identity that maintains continuity

---

[1] Paul Stevens, *Aging Matters: Finding your calling for the rest of your life* (Eerdmans, Grand Rapids, 2016) 1.

[2] Camilla Cavendish, *Extra Time: Ten lessons for an ageing world* (Harper Collins, London, 2019) 33.

[3] Tim Stafford, *As Our Years Increase* (British edition: IVP, Leicester, 1989), 12.

despite the physiological and social changes that come with age'.[4]

This is the context in which today's seniors want to be valued and treated with respect. Seniors still have much to offer. They also have great potential for further growth. In the words of a manifesto for old age drawn up by Julia Neuberger entitled, *Not Dead Yet*.

> Don't make any assumptions about my age.
> Don't waste my skills and experience.
> Don't take away my pride.
> Don't trap me at home.
> Don't make me brain dead, let me grow.
> Don't force me into a care home.
> Don't treat those who look after me as rubbish.
> Don't treat me like I'm not worth repairing.
> Don't treat my death as meaningless.
> Don't assume I'm not enjoying life.[5]

Many churches – including not least their ministers – need to repent of their ageism, which has caused them to see seniors as weak and dependent people who need to be helped and entertained. As Arthur Creber wrote:

> It really cannot be satisfactory for us to present a gospel which encourages older people to withdraw from life and to prepare for death (although this may be wholly appropriate for a person suffering from a terminal illness). Neither is it satisfactory to reduce our ministry to the patronising provision of free hand-outs or cheap trips to the pantomime at Christmas. If the gospel has to do with new Life, we should be encouraging older people to explore their potential for creative activity, for maintaining and improving their health, and for establishing or re-establishing loving relationships with other people and with God. We should be providing opportunities for the development of understanding, growth and experimentation. A positive approach to the potentialities of old age will motivate us as ministers and will ensure that

---

[4] Sharon Kaufmann quoted by Michael Butler and Ann Orbach, *Being Your Age* (SPCK, London, 1993), 13.
[5] Julia Neuberger, *Not Dead Yet: A Manifesto for Old Age* (HarperCollins, London, 2008).

the necessary resources are made available for the provision of creative opportunities.[6]

While in many churches there are meetings or clubs for older people, in few churches is there any strategy toward helping senior adults grow and develop. Pastoral care of senior adults is much more than keeping the 'old folk' happy. It is more than visiting the housebound and taking them communion. Pastoral care of senior adults lends itself to developing all kinds of innovative ministries, which enable people to grow and develop.

Ministers need to realise that their older members are never too old to learn. As Gordon Harris argued, 'Jethro, the father-in-law of Moses, Moses himself, Joshua, Caleb, Barzillai, the older counsellors of Rehoboam, Simeon, Anna, and early Jewish rabbis represent the best in lifelong learning. Lessons from these examples, undergirded by a high view of the potential of God's greatest creation, present a demanding challenge for growth to the older generation'.[7] I shall never forget meeting a distinguished American emeritus professor in church history, then in his late 70s, who at one point in our conversation said, 'Yes, in that particular area I've still got a lot of growing to do'. As one who was then in his late 40s, I felt challenged and asked myself: 'When I am in my late 70s will I still be in the business of growing?'

Now a senior myself, I too want to continue to grow and develop. For me reading helps me to keep my mind fresh. However, I also benefit from meeting with others, sharing and debating ideas, so that together we become more alive and more interesting as people. 'Iron sharpens iron, and one person sharpens the wits of another', says Prov. 27:17. Seniors in the church don't just need opportunities to socialise, they also need opportunities for theological reflection and stimulation. We are not just human beings, we are also human 'becomings'. According to Eugene Bianchi 'The greatest tragedy for a religious person is not being a sinner, but the embracing of stagnation, the refusal to grow'.[8] Many of us seniors want to continue to grow — leaders of today's churches please take note!

---

[6] Arthur Creber, *New Approaches to Ministry with Older People*, 23.
[7] J. Gordon Harris, *Biblical Perspectives on Aging: God and the Elderly* (Hawarth/Taylor & Francis, New York, 2nd edition, 2008), 158-159.
[8] Quoted by Paul Stevens, *Aging*, 143.

FUNERALS ARE MULTI-FACETED

As a young minister I believed that tributes at a funeral were wrong. A Christian funeral was not a place for eulogies, but for preaching. My task was to speak about the grace of God, and not about the departed. I followed William Carey's instructions for his own funeral: 'Speak not of Carey, speak of Carey's Saviour'.[1] I never encouraged tributes from friends and relatives. Instead, I would say a few words about their loved one, before getting on with 'the real job' of speaking about Jesus. Eventually I changed my mind. I now believe there is a place for tributes. For many years I have had a 'tribute slot' when one or two family members or friends have shared memories of the deceased.

Why the change of mind? Perhaps because I now see a distinction between a eulogy and a tribute. Although technically a 'eulogy' means only 'a speaking well', all too often it involves an exercise in praise so unreal that it contravenes the Trades Description Act. In a Christian funeral there is no place for such a glorification of the departed – for 'all have sinned and fall short of the glory of God' (Rom. 3:23). Along with our virtues we have our vices. I have therefore asked that at my funeral the sermon text be taken from 2 Cor. 4:7: 'We have this treasure in clay jars, so that it may be made clear that this extraordinary power belongs to God and does not come from us.'

Although in the introduction to my sermon at a funeral I normally say a few words about the deceased, I tend to keep my tribute short. As I discovered on one memorable occasion, it is

---

[1] See S. Pearce Carey, *William Carey* (Hodder & Stoughton, London, 1923), 375. He instructed that on his tombstone, along with his name and dates, there should be just a couplet from Isaac Watts: 'A wretched, poor and helpless worm/On Thy kind arms I fall' (*William Carey* 385).

possible to get things wrong. It was a funeral of a lady, who I had
only really known in the closing stages of her life. I thought she was
a wonderful Christian lady and told the congregation so – only to
discover at the funeral tea that there had been a mean and unkind
streak to her character. I am now much more careful in what I
say. As a Christian minister I cannot afford to engage in unreal
eulogising, for it then calls into question my own integrity, which
in turn could give the congregation reason to be sceptical about my
affirmations of the Gospel.

So what then is involved in a funeral? It is a celebration of a life.
It is also an opportunity to speak about the difference that Jesus
makes to living and to dying, and to minister the grace of God into
the lives of those who mourn. A Christian funeral always involves
listening to Scripture: at my own funeral I have asked that Ps. 23,
John 14:1,2, 6; and 1 Cor. 15:20, 42-44, 51-57 be read. And there
are the prayers, where we praise God for the Gospel, thank God
for the deceased, and pray for those who mourn.

Over the years I developed a 'standard' sermon for when I took
funerals of non-Christians with no church association, which I then
'tweaked' as appropriate. I said:

> Death finds us at our most religious. Many no longer mark
> birth of a child with any religious ceremony – likewise most
> people no longer bother to go to church to be married. But
> few people do without a minister or priest at the point of
> death. Why is this so? Why don't we dispense with all the
> religious paraphernalia and hold a secular or humanist
> ceremony instead? Let me give three good reasons for holding
> a Christian funeral service:
>
> 1. Today we come to thank God for the life of our loved one.
> Sadly, I never knew (name), but let me encourage you to
> allow some of your memories to surface and then be grateful
> to God for them. For God is 'the giver of every good and
> perfect gift' (Jas. 1:17 AV). So, look back and be grateful to
> God for all that (name) was to you.
>
> 2. Today we come to receive the comfort that God alone can
> offer. Death is always a troubling event, however expected

it may have been. Alas for the person without faith all one can do is to maintain a stiff upper lip. Death is the end: it is literally 'curtains' as the crematorium curtains are pulled over. But where there is faith there is hope. As the Apostle Paul said, 'When the body is buried it is mortal; when raised it is immortal. When buried it is ugly and weak; when raised it will be beautiful and strong. When buried it is a physical body; when raised it will be a spiritual body' (1 Cor. 15:42-44 GNB). How do we know that this is not just wishful thinking? Because of what Jesus has done. Jesus has broken through death's defences. He has carved out a path through the valley of death and through faith we may follow in his steps. So here at the point of death comfort is to be found. Death need not have the last word.

3. Today we come to ask God for strength to cope. The God and Father of our Lord Jesus Christ does not live in some remote ivory tower. He didn't set the world in motion and then withdraw from the scene. Rather, he is involved in the everyday processes of life. The Psalmist in one of our readings said: 'He gives me new strength. He guides me in the right way' (Ps. 23:3 GNB). He goes with us even through the valley of death. God is with us at every point of our living and of our dying. My prayer for you all is that you will open yourselves to experience the strength that God alone can give.

Christian funerals are, of course, different in character from non-Christian funerals. Inevitably we celebrate not just the life of the deceased, but also the new life which is theirs in Christ. However, there must be also an opportunity for people to express their grief. I am concerned that today this aspect of the funeral is missing in many churches. Some years ago, I went to the funeral of a great friend who died far too young, with still so much to offer. I was devastated by his death and by its suddenness – only two weeks from diagnosis of cancer to death. I arrived for the service very much a mourner, but alas, was given no room to mourn. The funeral was billed as a 'Service of Celebration and Thanksgiving'. From start to finish celebration and thanksgiving were the order of the day. Apart from the preacher, nobody mentioned the word 'pain' or 'sorrow'. Instead, we were called to rejoice in the triumph of the risen Christ and in the hope of resurrection which is ours. The hymns and songs were all upbeat, with a worship band accompanying the organ. It was toe-tapping, hand-raising stuff. I felt even more miserable. I wanted to cry, but nobody addressed my pain. I, a staunch Nonconformist, found myself longing for a requiem mass!

The reality is that death is a nasty business. Death is not to be trivialised. Job described death as 'the king of terrors' (Job 18:14). The Psalmist was equally realistic: 'My heart is in anguish within me, the terrors of death have fallen upon me. Fear and trembling come upon me, and horror overwhelms me' (Ps. 55:4-5). Even Paul, in his great chapter on the resurrection, called death 'the last enemy' (1 Cor. 15:25). We believe in resurrection, but resurrection presupposes death. If we are to be true to life, then we need to acknowledge the pain, the bleakness, and the sheer utter 'bloodiness' of the situation. We do people no favours if we seek to protect them from the pain. I find it significant that on the very occasion when Jesus spoke of himself as the resurrection and the life (John 11:25), 'Jesus wept' for his friend Lazarus (John 11:35). If Jesus could weep, then so too may we. If the bereaved are not given an opportunity to acknowledge their pain and loss, then the grieving process may take so much longer.[2]

Allowing people to grieve does not mean that there is no place for celebration. Although we may weep for our loss, we need not weep for those who have died in Christ. They are safe in the Father's house (John 14:1-2). Death for them is 'gain' (Phil. 1:21). I love John Bunyan's description of Mr Valiant-for-Truth's dying:

> After this it was noised abroad, that Mister Valiant-for-Truth was taken with a summons and had this for a token

---

[2] See Nick Watson, *Preaching at Funerals: How to Embed the Gospel in Funeral Ministry* (Grove, Cambridge, 2nd edition 2019) 10: 'I would ... counsel and care that whatever we preach, and whatever we do liturgically at a funeral, does not reinforce our society's preference to minimise the pain of bereavement. Too much language helps avoid acknowledging the impact of death. "Passed on", "fallen asleep", "departed" are all easier to face than "dead". The use of oblique language is more widespread. I have noticed increasingly that printed orders of service are titled "Thanksgiving for the life of ..." rather than "Funeral of ...".'

that the summons was true, 'That his pitcher was broken at the fountain'. Then said he, I am going to my Father's; and though with great difficulty I am got hither, yet now I do not repent me of all the trouble I have been at to arrive where I am. My sword, I give to him that shall succeed me in my pilgrimage, and my courage and skill, to him that can get it. My marks and scars I carry with me, to be a witness for me, that I have fought His battles, who now will be my rewarder. When the day that he must go hence was come, many accompanied him to the river-side, into which as he went, he said, 'Death, where is thy sting?', and as he went down deeper, 'Grave, where is thy victory?' So he passed over, and all the trumpets sounded for him on the other side.[3]

In the light of the resurrection hope, there is a place for the sounding of trumpets on this side too. Death is a *defeated* enemy! Paul was right to declare: 'Thanks be to God who gives us the victory through our Lord Jesus Christ' (1 Cor. 15:56). Not to celebrate the difference that Jesus makes to living and to dying would be a denial of our faith. But in our funeral sermons and liturgies we need to allow people to grieve as well as to celebrate.

3 John Bunyan, *The Pilgrim's Progress* (first published, Part I 1678, Part II 1884; also Collins, London 1953), 317.

WORSHIP IS BOTH AN ART AND A SCIENCE

The writer to the Hebrews describes Jesus as a 'liturgist' (*leitourgos*): as our high priest he is 'a minister in the sanctuary' (Heb. 8:2) i.e. he serves in the worship of God. The root etymological meaning of our English word 'liturgy' is 'the public worship of God'. Liturgy has nothing to do with a particular form of words: it simply denotes the worship which we offer to God. 'Into the liturgy the people bring their entire existence so that it may be gathered up in praise. From the liturgy the people depart with a renewed vision of the value-patterns of God's kingdom, by the more effective practice of which they intend to glorify God in their whole life.'[1] This is the context I believe ministers are called to be 'creative liturgists'; they are called to lead their people into the presence of God himself.

Today, worship has become one of the great divides in church life. The term 'liturgical' has come to be equated with formal worship, such as is to be found among Anglicans and Roman Catholics, where the worship is ordered by a prayer book, although since the introduction of *Common Worship* in 2000 Anglican worship has become much more flexible and diverse within the 'common' Anglican framework of worship.[2] By contrast in the 'non-liturgical' churches worship is 'free', with no set orders to follow or set prayers to say.[3] But there are many other sub-divides

---

[1] Geoffrey Wainwright, *Doxology: A Systematic Theology* (Epworth, London, 1980), 8.

[2] A sign of this change is that in contrast to the one volume *Book of Common Prayer*, *Common Worship* is made up of twelve volumes, including material both 'authorised' and 'commended'. In the words of Phillip Tovey, *Common Worship* has become 'a rich resource to help congregations worship God through the Spirit' (*Mapping Common Worship*, Grove, Cambridge, 2008), 3.

[3] As Christopher Ellis, *Gathering: A Theology and Spirituality of Worship in Free Church Tradition* (SCM, London, 2004) has pointed out, in Free Church worship, when prayer books are used, 'they will be a resource for those leading worship rather than a centrally authorised set of words in the hands of the congregation. Each service will be different, using an infinitely variable mixture of hymns and extempore and specially written prayers'.

too: in addition to 'classic worship', an online worship forum listed other classifications such as 'multisensory worship', 'indigenous worship', 'innovative worship', 'transformational worship', 'blended worship', 'praise services', 'spirited traditional' and 'creative worship'![4]

Over the years there have been massive changes to the way in which many churches approached worship. There was a time when preaching was exalted above everything else, and worship belonged to the 'preliminaries', while the celebration of the Lord's Supper was an addendum to the main service. For British Baptists things changed radically with the so-called 'liturgical renewal' of the 1950s, and as a result worship became more important, and the Lord's Supper became an integral part of the service. At that stage ministers still did almost everything in the service: church members might be invited to read the Scriptures or lead the prayers of intercession, but the service itself was structured and led by the minister. Then in the mid-1960s came 'charismatic renewal' and the structures of worship were blown apart: informality and openness became the norm. In many churches today the minister just preaches the sermon, while the 'worship' group, often an enthusiastic band of guitar-strumming young people, will be responsible for leading the worship.

In principle the thawing of God's 'frozen' people[5] is to be welcomed. Today it can feel both strange and unnatural to lead a service of worship without active congregational participation. Worship that involves others in both the planning and the executing is always richer than anything a 'one-man band' can offer. Yet such worship has its dangers. For although there may be no one pattern of worship, there are principles that lie behind it. Worship is both an art and a science. It is not sufficient to be gifted in leading worship: such a gift needs to be trained and developed. Ministers, precisely because of their training, still have overall responsibility

---

[4] See Melanie C. Ross, *Evangelical versus Liturgical? Defying a Dichotomy* (Eerdmans, Grand Rapids, 2014), 134. As a generalisation, Ross noted that in the USA evangelicals have adopted a frontier '*ordo*', with its threefold shape of preliminary songs that 'soften up' an audience, a fervent sermon, and an altar call for new converts, and the effective marginalisation of the Eucharist. By contrast, churches with a liturgical tradition have a fourfold order rooted in the four primary symbols of word, bath, table and prayer (*Evangelical versus Liturgical?* 6).

[5] The expression is taken from *God's Frozen People* (Collins, London, 1965) by Mark Gibbs and T. Ralph Martin, a seminal book 'about – and for – ordinary Christians'.

for the worship of the church.

The British Baptist editors of *Patterns and Prayers for Christian Worship* had some wise things to say about 'competent guidance':

> Evangelical worship can lose its sense of direction. The idea of movement implicit in some of the traditional orders of service needs to be retained. God has indeed poured out his Spirit upon his people in a new way. Many pastors have abdicated their traditional role of leading worship and handed it over to the church's musicians. Yet there is a clear difference between leading songs and leading worship. To lead a congregation in worship is to be entrusted with one of the most important tasks of the church. Those who lead acts of worship in which many participate require:
>
> - The training and development of gifts
> - The ability to guide the service in order to avoid crosscurrents of emotion and ambition
> - Structures to include praise, proclamation and prayer
> - Direction to move the people on sensitively and expectantly
> - Strength to provide confidence and security.[6]

Although I myself was very much part of the heady days of charismatic renewal, I remain convinced that ultimately the responsibility for worship lies with the ordained ministers of God's people.[7] It is precisely because of this responsibility that ministers receive training in the leadership of worship.

This does not mean to say that the leading of worship should be the exclusive preserve of the trained minister. That is not a good thing. There is a real danger of 'sameness' if the worship is solely in the hands of one person. Where there are a variety of worship leaders, there can be a variety of patterns of worship. Yet even where others are involved, ultimately the minister is responsible for the conduct of worship. It is with the minister that 'the buck' stops.

This is not a plea to return to old formats of worship, but rather a plea for ministers to re-discover their role as 'creative

---

[6] Bernard Green et al (eds.), *Patterns and Prayers for Christian Worship: A guide-book for worship leaders* (Oxford University Press, 1991), 7.
[7] *Patterns and Prayers for Christian Worship*, 187, 190.

liturgists'.[8] Alas, in many evangelical churches today ministers along with their worship leaders have failed to see the need for creativity. Australians Michael Frost and Alan Hirsch, reflecting on their world tour of churches, commented that one of their lasting impressions was that churches 'tended to be invariably dull and rather predictable. They had a disturbing propensity to look, feel, and act in basically the same way. They sang the same basic songs and followed the same basic order of service in their corporate worship. The sheer predictability of it all was quite shocking and deeply disturbing'.[9] If worship is to be truly satisfying, if worship is to lead into the presence of God, if worship is to provide the norms and inspiration for living, then ministers in partnership with their worship leaders and musicians must take responsibility for the structure and direction of worship.

---

[8] For ideas, see Paul Beasley-Murray, *Living out the Call: Serving the People of God*, 30-53.
[9] Michael Frost and Alan Hirsch, *The Shaping of Things To Come*, 182.

SPIRIT-LED PRAYERS IN PUBLIC WORSHIP ARE BEST PREPARED

I was going to entitle this lesson 'Spirit-led prayers in public worship are rarely extempore', but on reflection felt that was too provocative. However, what I am wishing to counter is the sloppiness in much non-liturgical public worship which counts for prayer. To quote Andrew Walker and Robin Parry in their superb book, *Deep Church Rising*:

> To extemporise prayer is often to dig into a compendium of well-worn religious clichés strung together with as much familiarity and repetition as monks reciting the Office together, or a sisterhood of nuns telling the rosary. Extempore prayers can be personal and profound, but they can also be hackneyed and shallow. Because God is a good God, we are absolutely not saying that he does not hear these prayers, but we are arguing that tossing out thoughts to heaven can betray a certain laziness of mind and an absence of spiritual discipline.[1]

Furthermore, modern research has revealed that extempore prayer is not as free as some proponents realise. In the words of Lester Ruth, an American Methodist scholar: 'Typically the one praying will draw upon several repertories of formulas, phrases and clichés to create the prayer, especially biblical quotes and allusions, phrases central to the piety of the one who prays, and standardised indicators of internal structure and transition.'[2]

---

[1] Andrew G. Walker and Robin A. Parry, *Deep Church Rising: Recovering the roots of Christian orthodoxy* (SPCK, London, 2014), 107.
[2] Paul Bradshaw 'Extempore Prayer' in *The New SCM Dictionary of Liturgy and Worship* (SCM, London, 2002).

But before I develop my argument, we need first to define what we mean by extempore prayer. The word is derived from a Latin phrase *ex tempore* which literally means 'from or out of time'. It is praying without premeditation or preparation. It is praying 'on the spur of the moment', 'off-the cuff' praying. One proof-text for such an approach is found in Mark 13:11: 'Do not worry beforehand about what you are to say; but say whatever is given you at that time, for it is not you who speak, but the Holy Spirit.' But the context here is very different: it refers not to prayer but to Christians defending themselves in court. To equate the Spirit with the spontaneous is wrong. Indeed, on that basis we would have to excise the Psalms from Scripture, for many of them are most certainly not spontaneous prayers to God, but rather carefully constructed literary compositions. Another proof text drawn upon is 2 Cor. 3:17: 'Where the Spirit of the Lord is, there is freedom', but the freedom relates to salvation, and not worship.

Secondly, I need to make clear that I am not arguing for set liturgical prayers over against extempore prayer. In my retirement I am currently worshipping in an Anglican cathedral, where I am enjoying the richness and variety of Anglican collects and other set Anglican prayers – but that is not the issue. The issue for me is that prayer that is offered in public worship should normally be prayer that has been carefully thought through. Jesus calls us, in the words of the *Shema*, to love the Lord our God 'with all our mind' as well as 'with all our heart and with all our soul' (Matt. 22:27) – and that should be also true of our public praying. Isaac Watts, for instance, wrote of 'conceived' prayer 'done by some work of meditation before we begin to speak in prayer', as distinct from extempore prayer 'when we without any reflection or meditation beforehand address ourselves to God and speak the thoughts of our hearts as fast as we can conceive them'.[3]

Precisely how we think through our praying can vary. As a young minister I sometimes just used headings; at other times I made full notes, while occasionally I would write out my prayers in full. Later in my ministry I always wrote out my prayers in full. I came to feel that God deserved my very best: or in the words of David,

[3] *Isaac Watts, Guide to Prayer* (1715) quoted by Stephen Winward, *Responsive Prayers and Praises for Minister and Congregation* (Hodder & Stoughton, London, 1981), 3.

'I will not offer to the Lord my God sacrifices that which cost me nothing' (2 Sam. 24:24 GNB). It is not that I cannot extemporise in prayer. Far from it, I can 'fly by the seat of my pants' when it comes to public prayer as well as anyone, but that is not God-honouring. Indeed, I would argue that my prepared prayers now are probably more truly Spirit-led.

Notice too that 'preconceived' or 'prepared' prayers are still forms of free prayer. They are not set prayers, which, although they may have beauty, inevitably lack particularity. No set prayer can ever be perfectly suited to every occasion: there is always a certain generality of expression. Nor is it true that read prayers lack warmth and become more artificial in feeling: as I read my prayers I am still pouring out my heart and soul to God. Nor is there no room for the spontaneous when prayers have been prepared: there is nothing to stop me breaking away from my text if God suddenly lays something on my heart. Significantly, I have discovered that the more I have prepared my prayers, the more people are likely to thank me for my praying.

Again, let me make clear, that I am not against extempore prayer. Most of my praying is spontaneous. As a child, apart from the Lord's Prayer, I never learnt any set prayers. Nor when I was a parent did I ever teach any prayers to my children. Personal prayer for me has always been extempore prayer; and so it continues to be. In my daily 'quiet times' my praying is a form of conversation with God. Similarly, in the context of counselling or visiting my prayers are extempore. At the end of a pastoral conversation I do not pull out a prayer book, but simply and naturally lead in a prayer in which I bring before God the concerns that have been expressed. Likewise, for me extempore prayer has always been the norm in the context both of home groups and the many other meetings which are part of church life. I agree with Stephen Winward, a Baptist minister of my father's generation, who said: 'Warm, direct, intimate, personal extempore prayer corresponds to the nature of prayer as conversation with God.'[4]

However, while extempore prayer may be the order of the day in the home or the prayer meeting, there is much to be said for

---

[4] Stephen Winward, *Celebration and Order* (Baptist Union of Great Britain, London 1981), 28.

prepared prayer in public services of worship. In my experience although in theory Baptists and others in a non-liturgical tradition are free to produce the very best of prayers, they are also free to abuse their freedom and produce the third-rate. Prayer needs to be Spirit-led, but that is not necessarily extempore!

GREAT WORSHIP CLIMAXES AROUND THE LORD'S TABLE

The highpoint for Christian worship must surely be the celebration of the Lord's Supper. Indeed, I would argue along with Roman Catholics and Anglicans that the Lord's Supper should be the central act of worship in the church. It is significant that Paul's teaching on the Lord's Supper is given in a context where he is speaking of what takes place when the Corinthians 'come together as a church' (1 Cor. 11:18). Likewise, at Troas the Lord's Supper was celebrated once a week: 'on the first day of the week,' records Luke, 'we came together to break bread' (Acts 20:7). In the church in Jerusalem it was one of the four key components of their worship: 'They devoted themselves to the apostles' teaching and fellowship, to the breaking of bread and the prayers' (Acts 2:42).

Unfortunately, the Lord's Supper is yet to become truly central in many non-liturgical churches. Baptists, for instance, for all their desire to honour the Scriptures and follow its teaching, are for the most part non-sacramental in their worship.[1] Maybe they need to take note of John Calvin, who regarded infrequent communion as 'an invention of the devil'. The French Reformed scholar, J. J. von Allmen, was of the decided opinion that 'the absence of the Eucharist shows contempt for grace'.[2]

When Baptists do have communion, they often find it difficult to truly celebrate the faith. The emphasis is on remembering Jesus and his cross. However, in the early church the focus was also on

---

[1] Christopher Ellis in *Gathering* (pp. 191-2) suggested that Baptist resistance to more frequent celebrations of the Supper 'may partly be because the quietism of the service is at odds with the upbeat mood of much Sunday worship. Like many evangelicals, they are determinedly activist and the reflective and unvaried nature of the Supper may only be sustainable on a monthly basis.'

[2] J. J. von Allmen, *Worship: Its Theology and Practice* (Lutterworth, London, 1965), 156.

the Risen Lord. We see this in the expression 'the Lord's Supper' (1 Cor. 11:20), where the adjective translated as 'the Lord's' (*kuriakos*) is derived from the Greek noun *Kurios*, the title the first Christians used for the risen and ascended Lord: it is 'the name above every name' which God gave to Jesus when he 'highly exalted him' (Phil 2:9-11).[3] At the Lord's Table, therefore, we are called not just to remember the Crucified Saviour, but to encounter the Risen Lord. We may not believe in the Roman Catholic doctrine of the 'real presence' of Christ, and yet, as the Emmaus couple discovered, Christ is truly present amongst us as we break bread and drink wine (Luke 24:30-31). Furthermore, this risen Lord Jesus has promised to return in glory: indeed, the apostle Paul calls us to 'proclaim the Lord's death until he comes' (1 Cor. 11:26). The Lord's Supper is an anticipation of the Marriage Supper of the Lamb (see Matt. 26:29), when there shall be an end to suffering and to death; when we shall be reunited with our loved ones and all God's people; and when, above all, we shall be united with God himself (Rev. 21:3-4).

Rightly understood, the Lord's Supper is a meal with a multiple focus on Jesus:

- At the invitation of the Lord all who love him and desire to follow him come to eat, and drink.
- Under the authority of the Lord we reaffirm at the Table our baptismal vows to die to self and to live for him.
- In memory of the Crucified Lord we remember his death and the love that took him to Calvary.
- In the presence of the Risen Lord we encounter him in the breaking of the bread.
- In celebration of the Returning Lord we look forward to the day when every knee will bow and every tongue will confess that Jesus is Lord to the glory of God the Father.

The Lord's Supper calls for celebration. The question arises: how can this note of celebration be blended with the serious and sombre task of remembering? Alas, in many Baptist churches, almost

---

[3] *Kuriakos* is found in only one other place in New Testament: Rev 1:10. There it is used of the 'Lord's day', the day when Christians celebrated the resurrection of Jesus from the dead.

immediately after the bread and wine have been served, the service is brought to a hasty end, with little if any time allowed for the necessary journey from the cross to the resurrection and beyond. Time needs to be made for worship to build up and to come to a climax – not least in a final hymn of triumph to the risen, ascended and reigning Lord Jesus.

But there is a more serious development taking place in many evangelical churches committed to the development of contemporary worship, and that is what I can only call 'the dumbing down' of communion. In some churches communion has become a 'self-service buffet', where worshippers just help themselves to bread and wine – or, as in the case of one American church, Kool-Aid and cheese crackers. Ben Witherington tells of how at this American church, a visiting 'seeker' went up to the senior minister after the service and said: 'You know what I really liked about the service?' 'No', the minister answered. 'I liked it that, in the middle, we stopped and had snacks.' Reflecting on this encounter, the minister said later, 'An unacceptable image arose in my mind during this conversation: "This is my snack, given for you." The Lord's Supper had been trivialised. Indeed, comments Witherington, 'some would say that sacrilege happened that day in that church'.[4]

This is not an extreme one-off case. The phenomenon of 'fast food worship, welcome to MacEucharist' is not unusual.[5] Mark Galli, the editor-in-chief of *Christianity Today* wrote: 'I've lost track of the number of startup evangelical churches whose practice of Communion is frankly a sacrilege. One has to give them credit for seeking out the lost and taking down unnecessary cultural and religious barriers. And one has to also praise them for at least offering Communion. But in many churches, it is something that is presented during the offering, at a small table holding crackers and juice on the side aisles for those who feel so led to partake. Sometimes this is accompanied by the words of institution, but sometimes not.'[6] In many churches there is no longer a formal

---

[4] Witherington, *We Have Seen His Glory*, 147, 148.
[5] Walker & Parry, *Deep Church Rising*, 146.
[6] Mark Galli, 'Whatever happened to Communion and Baptism? Or why aren't we doing what Jesus told us to?', *Christianity Today*, July 2019.

corporate prayer of thanksgiving for God's salvation symbolised in bread and wine. In some churches instead of one central communion table, there are a host of small tables to which people are invited to go and help themselves to bread and wine. In one church I worshipped at there was no table, instead the bread and wine were put on the floor; while in another church the bread and wine were taken out of a drawer!

In many churches the Lord's Supper is no longer the climax to worship, but is squeezed into the main service before the sermon. Yet if we wish to pattern ourselves on the early church, then the death of the Lord needs to be proclaimed before we eat bread and wine; the good news of Jesus needs to be preached from the Scriptures – otherwise there is a danger that the eating of bread and the drinking of wine becomes an empty rite.[7] Even where the Lord's Supper follows the sermon, there is no guarantee that it has meaning. Some years ago, I was present at a service in a large Baptist church where immediately after the bread and wine had been served in a most cursory manner, the minister on draining his cup declared, 'The service is over. You are all invited to have a cup of tea in the hall at the back of the church.' There was no pastoral prayer for the needs of the fellowship (as has been customary in Baptist churches), no final hymn of triumph, no benediction or sharing of the Grace together. We had just 'done' communion! We had eaten bread and wine, but I doubt whether many of us that day had met with the Lord. I am not against change, for change is both inevitable and necessary; but where change involves throwing the baby out with the bathwater, then such change needs to be resisted.[8]

What can be done? In the first place, ministers should preach and teach more about the Lord's Supper. Even among Christians of long-standing there is widespread ignorance of what should be going through their minds as they take part in the Lord's Supper. New Christians in particular need instruction.[9]

---

[7] When Paul writes: 'For as often you eat this bread and drink the cup, you proclaim the Lord's death until he comes' (1 Cor. 11:26) he was not referring to the acts of eating and drinking, but to the telling of the story of the salvation that Jesus brings, just as Jews coming together for the Passover meal listened first to the story of their salvation as embodied in figures such as Abraham and Moses.
[8] For non-Anglicans wanting to enrich their communion services, see Nick Fawcett, *For You and for Many: Contemporary additional texts for celebrating the Lord's Supper* (Kevin Mayhew, Stowmarket, 2004).
[9] Paul Beasley-Murray, *Baptism, Belonging and Breaking of Bread: Preparing for Baptism* (Baptist Union of Great Britain, Didcot, 2010).

Ministers need also to help their people understand that the Lord's Supper has its origins in a meal: the Greek word translated 'supper' (*deipnon*) was used to denote the main meal of the day: 'He welcomes us to have fellowship or communion with him over this meal. Jesus calls us to eat with him and to do so not as individuals alone together like customers in McDonald's but as a family at table. It really is a meal of "Holy *Communion*".'[10] What is more, this service of Communion is not just an 'ordinance' laid down by our Lord for us to observe, but a 'sacrament', a 'means of grace' by which the Lord Jesus blesses us with his very self. Ministers need to help their people to reflect on what it means to feed on Christ by faith (John 6:54). To quote Andrew Walker and Robin Parry again:

> When you eat or drink something it enters right into the depths of you – it brings you life – it becomes part of you … Jesus speaks of drinking his blood and eating his flesh as a metaphor for taking his very life deep into our own spiritual lives by faith. We are united with him – his life becomes our life.[11]

---

[10] Walker & Parry, *Deep Church Rising*, 152.
[11] Walker & Parry, *Deep Church Rising*, 156.

GOOD PREACHING ENTAILS STRUCTURED SIMPLICITY

Preaching is at the heart of ministry. According to Eugene Peterson, it is the 'one thing needful' for any minister: 'Lest the "one thing" get buried in the frenzy of multi-tasking, we need continual reaffirmation of the "one thing" as both glory and mystery anchors our vocation.'[1] Peter Forsyth, a Scottish theologian of a former generation, declared: 'With its preaching Christianity stands or falls.'[2] More recently Michael Quicke wrote: 'If it were possible to run a spiritual seismometer over Christian history to record its major tremors, every quake would correspond to a renewed sense of God's presence in preaching.'[3] Certainly, for Baptists and the Free Churches in general, preaching is ultimately where 'it' happens – where God is at work, transforming lives of individuals and of communities.

Although never a great fan of his sermons, I love Martyn Lloyd-Jones' description of preaching as 'logic on fire'. 'A theology which does not take fire, I maintain, is a defective theology; or at least the man's understanding of it is defective. Preaching is theology coming through a man who is on fire. A true understanding and experience of the Truth must lead to this. I say again that a man who can speak about these things dispassionately has no right whatsoever to be in a pulpit; and should never be allowed to enter one.'[4] Preaching involves a carefully reasoned argument, but at the

---

[1] Eugene Peterson in his preface to Darrell W. Johnson, *The Glory of Preaching: Participating in God's Transformation of the World* (IVP Academic, Downers Grove, Illinois, 2009).

[2] P. T. Forsyth, *Positive Preaching and the Modern Mind* (Independent Press, London, 1907), 1.

[3] Michael Quicke, *360 Degree Preaching: Hearing, Speaking, and Living the Word* (Paternoster, Carlisle, 2003), 32.

[4] Martyn Lloyd-Jones, *Preaching and Preachers* (Hodder & Stoughton, London, 1971), 97. The use of the term 'man' is of course dated.

same time there must be passion. A lifeless sermon should be a contradiction in terms. 'Proclamation,' declared Paul Scott Wilson, 'makes God the centre of the sermon and offers the fire of the Holy Spirit in transforming power.'[5]

Preaching is also, in the often-quoted words of Phillips Brooks, an expression of 'truth through personality' – not least in the sense that there is evidence that the preacher's own character has been shaped by his or her own experience of God.[6] Or as Ruthana Hooke has written, the sermon should be 'a moment in the liturgy when the preacher speaks her own words, not those inherited from the tradition', and seeks to show how the promise of the Gospel has 'first transformed her'. 'It is in large part the preacher's personal connection to text and tradition that listeners long for.'[7]

Preaching is not the only way in which God makes himself known. As James Dunn noted, the question 'How are they to believe in one of whom they never heard?' (Rom. 10:14) reflects a society 'where the chief means of mass communication was oral; communication of the gospel by written means is not yet envisaged'.[8] Derek Tidball, attacking the 'idolatry of the pulpit', made a similar point: 'Down the centuries God has clearly used other forms of communication as well as the sermon'. He instanced theological disputation and debate, as in the Reformation; Bible translation and the directed, unmediated use of scripture; dramatic enactments, such as those pioneered by the prophets; writing, such as contemporary evangelistic books, which take their cue from the Gospels; even visionary experiences and dreams, for which there is much biblical precedent'.[9] However, as Tidball acknowledged 'the sermon is a vital tool by which God speaks, but one among others'.[10]

Through the preaching of his Word there is an opportunity for God to speak to the congregation. However, preachers need to

[5] Paul Scott Wilson, *Setting Words on Fire: Putting God at the Center of the Sermon* (Abingdon, Nashville, 2008), 1.

[6] Phillips Brooks, *Lectures on Preaching* (H. R. Allenson, London 1877), 233.

[7] Ruthanna Hooke, 'The challenge of preaching', 450 in Martyn Percy (ed.), *The Study of Ministry* (SPCK, London, 2019).

[8] James D.G. Dunn, *Word Biblical Commentary: Romans 9-16* (Word, Dallas, 1998), 621.

[9] Derek Tidball, *Preacher, keep yourself from idols* (IVP, Nottingham, 2011), 32, 33.

[10] Tidball, *Preacher, keep yourself from idols*, 34. To give a personal example: the morning service I attended one Palm Sunday had no sermon; instead a mime artist presented the message of the Cross through the eyes of the centurion for almost thirty minutes – it was a powerful form of Gospel communication.

ensure that when they preach, people do indeed hear God speak to them. This means therefore that at the heart of my preaching is the exposition of God's Word. Richard Bewes, a former rector of All Souls Langham Place, London, observed: 'Plenty of preaching in the West today is of an entertaining, joke-ridden nature; it is as if the church and the theatre have neatly swapped roles. It is the theatre that tends now to take on the big themes that speak to the dilemmas of humanity, while the biggest-selling tapes at Christian conferences will often be from the speakers with the best jokes and banter.'[11] This is a travesty. My task as a preacher is to unpack God's word and relate it to the world of our hearers. I appreciate that preaching styles are always changing, and yet I can only say that I doubt whether I could have lasted as a preacher over all these years if I had not committed myself to expository preaching. Expository preaching has ensured that I remained fresh. In my experience when we conscientiously expound God's Word Sunday by Sunday, we discover that we are always finding new truths to impart. But left to our own devices, we soon run out of bright ideas. 'The preacher who expounds his own limited stock of ideas becomes deadly wearisome at last. The preacher who expounds the Bible has endless variety at his disposal. For no two texts say exactly the same thing.'[12]

But if people are to hear God speak, then the sermon also needs to be shaped in such a way, that God's Word is allowed maximum impact on our hearers. Only so will preaching become fixed in people's minds and hearts; only so will it become, in the best sense of the word, memorable. Preparing a sermon for me involves three stages: it involves listening to the voice of God in Scripture, listening to the voices in the world of today, and then fixing the listening process in a way which enables people to hear clearly what God would say to them through the preacher. Shaping the sermon is hard work.

There is no one God-given way in which sermons must be shaped. In some traditions a good sermon has three points together with an introduction and a conclusion. On the other hand, there is no reason why a sermon should not have four points or five

---

[11] Quoted by John Drane, *After McDonaldization: Mission, Ministry and Christian Discipleship in an Age of Uncertainty* (Darton, Longman and Todd, London, 2008), 115.
[12] James Stewart, *Preaching* (Hodder & Stoughton, London, 2nd edition), 96.

points, or two main points, each with two sub-points. Sermons assume many forms. The important thing is that the preacher does not engage in a leisurely discursive ramble, but rather that there is a structure which serves to ram home the points that need to be made on the basis of the Scripture for the day. Structure gives clarity to preaching. Napoleon is said to have had three commands for his messengers: 'Be clear! Be clear! Be clear!' Preachers too need to be crystal clear. Our congregations need to be able to leave the service under no illusion about what was said.

Structure gives purpose and power to preaching. It enables preachers to develop an argument and apply it so that there is only one conclusion. For preachers, like barristers, are advocates: they are seeking a verdict. Preaching is not about God and about twenty minutes. True preaching has a very definite purpose in mind. To that end, structured simplicity is required.

SERMON ENDINGS ARE KEY

Darrell Jones, a former pastor of First Baptist Church, Vancouver, and now a 'teaching fellow' at Regent College, Vancouver, wrote a wonderful introduction to preaching entitled *The Glory of Preaching: Participating in God's Transformation of the World*. There he stated:

> I believe that whenever human beings leave a preaching moment (a preaching-of-the-Word-of-God moment) they will do so with:
>
> - A clearer vision of the living God in Jesus (who according to himself is the subject of any text, and therefore, of any sermon on any text) [John 5:39; Luke 24:27,44];
> - A better understanding of the gospel of Jesus, the good news of what God has done, is doing and will do in Jesus;
> - An 'alternative reading of reality', a different, more redemptive way of understanding the concrete circumstances, challenges and fear in their lives;
> - A new way of thinking, feeling, acting and reacting shaped by the clearer vision, better understanding and alternative reading;
> - A new power enabling them to walk in the new reality into which the preached text has brought them.'[1]

But is that always true? For while there have been times when God has spoken powerfully to me, there have also occasions when I have gone to church and listened to a sermon, and, despite all my hopes, nothing seemed to happen. I have even been known to fall asleep

---

[1] Darrell Johnson, *The Glory of Preaching: Participating in God's Transformation of the World* (IVP Academic, Downers Grove, Illinois, 2009), 11.

in a sermon – and to my embarrassment I was sitting on the front row for all to see!

When nothing seems to happen, is that the fault of the preacher? Clearly not always. Sometimes it can be the fault of the congregation, who perhaps come with no sense of expectancy that God will speak. However, if preachers are honest, the fault is sometimes ours. We have skimped on our preparation and have come with no real word from God – no wonder our listeners were bored.

Sermons need to be properly prepared. This involves not just having an attention-grabbing introduction and a thoughtful middle, but also an ending that in one way or another calls for a response. It is often the last five minutes of a sermon which really count. In the words of Richard Baxter, the great seventeenth-century Puritan pastor of Kidderminster, the preacher's task is to 'screw God's truth into their minds.'[2]

Endings are vital. The final 10 per cent of a sermon either makes or mars the sermon. Aaron Percy, a professor at Wesley Seminary, Indiana, has likened ending a sermon to landing a plane, and with that metaphor in mind listed three mistakes preachers often make:[3]

1. Hope the sermon lands itself. Sermons like planes, don't land themselves. Without the preacher's attention, they crash, skid and thud.

2. Circle (and re-circle) the runway. If you don't know how to end the sermon, you might just preach it again. In my experience long sermons often contain a good deal of repetition.

3. Pick a new destination. The only thing people want more than to get on the plane is to get off the plane! Sermons can be similar. Just as no pilot decides on a new destination at the last moment, neither should the preacher add an unrelated aside, tangent, or anecdote before wrapping up. To this I would add, even without a new destination, make sure the flight is not too long: My PhD supervisor, F. F. Bruce, used to say that if preachers had anything

---

[2] Richard Baxter, *The Reformed Pastor* (first published 1656: Banner of Truth, Edinburgh, 1974), 160.
[3] Aaron Perry, 'The last five minutes of a sermon': seedbed.com/preachingcollective.

worthwhile to say, they could say it within twenty minutes; if they had nothing to say, then they would need at least forty minutes! On the other hand, a homily of just five or ten minutes rarely takes the listener very far.

So what is the secret of ending a sermon well? According to one American preacher, Joe La Guardia, 'Preachers who exert power in their conclusions rely on emotion and inspiration, usually bringing their audience to its feet and raising both voice and hands to inspire people to take action. Repetition, rhythm, singing, chanting, and (in some traditions) hooping are tools in this preacher's toolbox.'[4] While such an ending may perhaps work in some black churches, I can only say that it would not normally work in the churches I have known.

Ken Dykes, my old principal at the Northern Baptist College, Manchester, used to say, we should give as much attention to the last sentence of our sermons as the first sentence. He also advised us to use the word 'wondrous' in that final sentence!

Yet important as is the final sentence, I believe that the content of that final sentence should always contain good news. Preachers should never speak of Jesus without encouraging people to discover the difference that Jesus makes to living. Even in sermons intended primarily for God's people, there should be a challenge for people who have yet to surrender their lives to Jesus.

This came home to me when I was preparing a sermon on the words of Jesus about not throwing your pearls before swine (Matt. 6:7). In my initial draft I had written of 'the immense value of the Gospel' but had not invited my listeners to discover the good news for themselves. My text was not a natural springboard for preaching an evangelistic sermon: for Jesus was primarily urging his followers to be discerning when it came to sharing the good news of the Kingdom with others. However, conscious that in my congregation there were always people who had yet to commit themselves to Christ, I felt I had to include a 'Gospel word'. As a result, on the basis of this strange text I developed a three-fold challenge:

[4] Joe La Guardia, 'How do preachers end a sermon?', *Baptist News Global*, 13 August 2015.

1. A challenge to discover 'the precious gift' of all that Jesus offers.

2. A challenge to share this good news with friends and colleagues who might be receptive to our message.

3. A challenge to love even the hardened cynics, for love can melt even the hardest of hearts.

In the light of those three challenges I prepared three prayers of response which I then used to follow the sermon:

1. A prayer for those who have yet to discover the 'pearl of great price'. 'Lord Jesus, I now see the amazing difference you can make to my life. In you there is forgiveness for all that has been wrong in my life; in you there is meaning for living; and in you there is hope of life eternal. With great joy I open the door of my heart to you: come into my life and be my Saviour and my Lord – and I will gladly follow you all the days of my life.'

2. A prayer for those who find it difficult to share their faith: 'Lord Jesus, far from throwing pearls before pigs, all too often I fail to tell anybody of the difference you have made to my life. Forgive me for keeping the good news to myself. Help me to forget my shyness, so that when the time is right, I can tell friends and colleagues of your amazing love for me.'

3. A prayer for those who find it difficult to love those who are different to us. 'Lord Jesus, sometimes I find it difficult to love those who seem to stubbornly turn their backs upon you and your ways. Forgive me for my narrow heartedness. Help me to love – and in loving reflect your love to all.'

If a Scriptural justification for such an approach is required, then maybe it is the request some Greeks made to Philip: 'Sir, we would see Jesus' (John 12:21 AV). Over the years I have seen a good number of pulpits with such a plaque. What a challenge for any preacher – to let their hearers 'see Jesus'.

If congregations are to hear God speak, then sermon endings are key.[5]

---

[5] For some examples, see Paul Beasley-Murray, *Living out the Call: Reaching theWorld*, 73-75.

BAPTISMAL SERVICES PROVIDE GREAT OPPORTUNITIES FOR GOSPEL PREACHING

Gospel preaching was at the heart of the ministry of Jesus. Mark wrote: 'Jesus came to Galilee, proclaiming [AV 'preaching'] the good news of God, and saying, 'The time is fulfilled, and the kingdom of God has come near, repent and believe the good news' (Mark 1:14, 15). But how do preachers today find opportunities to engage in Gospel preaching? The answer is 'with difficulty'. In many churches the congregation is made up of the 'converted' rather than the 'unconverted', with the result that all too often Gospel preaching consists in telling 'the old, old story' to those already familiar with its message.

However, there are occasions in a church's life which can be turned into great opportunities for Gospel preaching. One such is a baptismal service. Yet, in my experience, these opportunities are not always grasped. In some churches the primary focus of a baptismal services is on those being baptised, with the result that the emphasis is on the call to discipleship rather than the call to repentance and faith.

This was the case when I along with eleven others was baptised in Zurich. With the River Limmat only a stone's throw away where the Swiss Reformer Ulrich Zwingli had drowned Anabaptist women on ducking stools and burnt Anabaptist men at the stake, we were reminded of the cost of discipleship. The baptisms were followed by the laying on of hands and then the Lord's Supper when for the first time I received bread and wine. Each one of us was given a special baptismal text. Mine was, 'If we live, we live to the Lord, and if we die, we die to the Lord; so then, whether we live or whether we die, we are the Lord's' (Rom. 14:8). For me as a thirteen-year old it was an overwhelmingly solemn and almost terrifying occasion. Significantly, although the church was well-attended, there were no 'guests' present. Strange as I now find it, it had never been suggested to me that I should invite any of my school friends along. The opportunity to preach the Gospel to those outside the confines of the church was lost. Instead, we had a theologically satisfying service with its primary focus on the Christian life.

Thankfully, there are many churches where the primary focus at a baptismal service is on calling men and women to faith. As a teenager I belonged to a church which under the leadership of a gifted evangelist was experiencing a mini-'revival' with the result that we seemed to have baptisms every month. At the end of every baptismal service the minister gave an 'altar call', and as we sang the six verses of 'Just as I am, without one plea', people streamed forward to give their lives to Christ – all ready to be baptised the following month!

Later, when I was a minister myself, I resolved to ensure that the baptismal services I led were outward-facing rather than inward-facing. I used to tell the baptismal candidates that it was their job to fill the church. I encouraged them to invite as many people as possible to their baptism. I got them to draw up lists of family members, friends, neighbours, colleagues, school friends. Many of my young people invited not just all their school class, but also their teachers too. We often had a hundred or more 'guests' present at a baptismal service. What a great opportunity I had for Gospel preaching!

And what great Scripture passages there are on which to preach on such an occasion. My favourites were:

1. Peter's response to the crowd in Jerusalem on the day of Pentecost: 'Repent and be baptised every one of you in the name of Jesus Christ so that your sins may be forgiven; and you will receive the gift of the Holy Spirit' (Acts 2:38).

2. Philip's encounter with the high-ranking Ethiopian official on the road from Jerusalem to Gaza. In response to the Ethiopian's request for baptism Philip said, 'If you believe with all your heart you may', and he replied, 'I believe that Jesus Christ is the Son of God' (Acts 8:37).

3. The answer of Paul and Silas to the Philippian jailer who wanted to know what he must do to be saved: 'Believe on the Lord Jesus, and you will be saved, you and your household' (Acts 16:31)

These and a host of other passages formed the basis of my baptismal preaching on countless occasions. What is more, the preaching was confirmed by the vibrancy of the worship, the testimonies given by the candidates, and the welcome given to the guests by the church.

As the years went by I found the task of preaching the Gospel on such occasions increasingly challenging, for it seemed to me that more and more of my hearers knew less and less of the presuppositions underlying the Gospel. With most children no longer attending Sunday School and the Christian faith no longer taught in our schools, more was needed than a one-off Gospel sermon at a baptismal service before meaningful commitment to Christ could take place. Often the response on such an occasion was simply a decision to learn more by attending an Alpha course. This is not to say that Gospel preaching has had its day. Rather, it is a call to engage more deeply in Gospel apologetics, as Paul did at Ephesus (Acts 19:8-10).

Baptismal services provide great opportunities for Gospel preaching, and not just within churches where believers' baptism is the norm. As one who in his retirement now worships in an Anglican church, I see too the opportunities present where infant baptism is practised. I find it surprising how many non-churchgoers still want their children 'done', and how many of their family and friends turn up for the baptisms. Here within this context the opportunities begin with preparing the parents for their child's baptism – as well as the preaching on the day itself. Although no advocate of infant baptism, I acknowledge that the opportunities for the Gospel are considerable.

But, and this is the issue, these opportunities need to be taken in every church. Just as Paul was driven to share the Good News with others – 'Woe to me if I do not proclaim the gospel' (1 Cor. 9:16) – so too we must be equally driven to make opportunities to share the Good News with others.

EVERY CHURCH IS DIFFERENT

That every church is different is to state the blindingly obvious. We don't have to go even further than the pages of the New Testament: the church at Jerusalem was very different from the church at Corinth, and the church in Ephesus was very different from the churches of Galatia. Similarly, the seven churches mentioned in the Book of Revelation all had their own distinctive character.

What was true in the first century remains true in the twenty-first century. Here I do not have in mind the vast array of theological and ecclesiological differences, but the differences within the same denomination or wing of the church, differences which have their roots in different experiences and histories. An analysis of the congregational dynamics of any given church involves eight different perspectives: personal faith stories; interpersonal networks and connections; numerical data; shared congregational history; surrounding community; espoused and operant theology; congregational dynamics; and oneself as leader.[1] Recognising that every church is unique, churches today are encouraged to engage in 'Mission Action Planning' which involves not only a review of the church and its vision for mission but also a community audit. There is no one way of sharing God's love with others, for every church and community are different.[2]

Certainly, the two churches of which I was minister were in some ways as different as cheese from chalk. True, when I arrived, both churches were in decline, but whereas my first church knew that change was necessary, many in my second church were not so

---

[1] See David Gortner, 'Congregational studies and ministry' 70-88 in Martyn Percy (ed.), *The Study of Ministry* (SPCK, London, 2019).
[2] See Mark Ireland and Mike Chew (eds.), *How to do Mission Action Planning: Prayer, Process and Practice* (SPCK, London, 2009).

sure. My first church was a very warm and loving church, whereas in my second church initially relationships left a lot to be desired – instead of talking through their differences, people sent letters to one another, and indeed to the minister (at one stage I received what I can only call 'hate mail'). In my first church everything I touched, as it were, immediately 'turned to gold': within a matter of months the church began to grow, young people abounded, and the giving increased so much that the budget had to be revised upwards. By contrast in my second church, although I adopted the same approach, everything I touched seemed to 'turn to dust' and for the first seven years the church continued to decline. The fact that I had already had thirteen years of ministry in Altrincham seemed to count for nothing when I came to Chelmsford: I had to learn so much more about ministry in order to turn that church around.

The fact is that every church has its own distinctive DNA. Something that has been tried and tested in one situation with good effect may not be appropriate in another situation. The style of ministry and mission at Saddleback or at Willowcreek, or at Holy Trinity Brompton or at All Souls cannot be transferred 'lock, stock and barrel' elsewhere. Every church has its own individual character and its own particular mission to fulfil. God is not in the business of cloning – and rightly so! Apart from anything else, every location is different: the needs and challenges of suburbia are very different from the needs and challenges of the inner city or of a large housing estate.

This does not mean to say that ministers and churches cannot learn from one another. 'Intelligent people are always and eager and ready to learn' (Prov. 18:15 GNB), words which the *Living Bible* translates as 'The intelligent man is always open to new ideas. In fact he looks for them'. Over the years I have greatly benefited from seeing how others operate and subsequently adapting the insights gained in my own church. So when I was minister at Altrincham, I spent a sabbatical in the States, which included doing a course on church growth taught by Peter Wagner, visiting churches, talking with church leaders, with a view to seeing what might work in my own situation. Later in Chelmsford I spent a three-month sabbatical visiting churches in New Zealand and Australia, and returned home with a host of new insights. However, I never simply 'adopted' what I saw, for to 'adopt' an idea from another church fails to recognise the unique character of each church. Rather the challenge was to see how an idea might be 'adapted'. We can learn from one another, provided we do not slavishly imitate. Each church has its own special calling to be church.

It is not only the churches which are different – ministers too are different. They have different gifts and abilities: one might be more of a pastor; another might be more of an evangelist or a community leader. Precisely because of those different gifts and abilities our callings may be very different from our predecessors or indeed successors. The wise church instead of comparing one minister with another, will welcome the different styles and approaches offered to them by their successive ministers.

It is not just churches that compare one minister with one another – ministers do this too. I have discovered that one of the temptations of ministry is to constantly compare oneself with other ministers, and in the process become envious of others and of the way in which God appears to be blessing others. Ministers need to focus on Jesus and not on others. In this regard we need to take notice of the rebuke Peter received after Jesus had said that the day would come when 'someone else will fasten a belt around you and take you where you do not want to go'. John tells us that, 'Peter turned and saw the disciple whom Jesus loved' and said to Jesus 'Lord, what about him?'. Jesus declared: 'If it is my will that he remain until I come, what is that to you? Follow me' (John 21:20-22). Our business is to follow Jesus and to fulfil our particular calling, and not to be concerned with anybody else.

MEANINGFUL FELLOWSHIP IS BEST EXPRESSED IN SMALL GROUPS

To my amazement I now find myself hosting and leading a fellowship group. Although as a minister I had often promoted and written material for such groups, until I 'retired' I had rarely hosted or led a group. I saw that as a job for others. But now that I am no longer leading a church, I am one of the 'others'. In some ways I feel privileged to be asked to care for a group – but I also feel somewhat challenged.

The group that I am leading has been going for some time, so I did not have the challenge of creating a group. However, I do have the challenge of developing the group. With that challenge in mind, at the beginning of my tenure as a group leader, I wrote to all the members of the group with a view not just to inviting them to my home, but also to setting out my aims. I said:

> There is more to a fellowship group than studying the Bible together. As the very name suggests, the key to a fellowship group is the fostering of community. If I were asked to sum up my ideal of a fellowship group, I would say:
>
> • Fellowship groups are about friendship, community, and sharing life together. They are places where people can relax with one another, laugh with one another, and even weep with one another: they are about being real with one another.
> • Fellowship groups are about caring for one another, being there for one another, praying for one another, and offering practical support for one another
> • Fellowship groups are about reading the Bible together and discovering how God's Word applies to our everyday lives.

- Fellowship groups are about encouraging one another to share the good news of Jesus with others.
- Fellowship groups are about extending friendship to others, and inviting others to join us, even if it means that in the end a new group has to divide to accommodate all the newcomers.

Hopefully, I have whetted your appetite to join us! And, of course, if you wish to bring a friend, please feel free to do so.'

I like the term 'fellowship group'. Other churches speak of 'small groups', 'Bible study groups', 'cell groups', 'nurture groups', or 'life groups'. However, 'fellowship group' describes most clearly their purpose: such groups are about developing a community, where people can love one another as brothers and sisters in Christ. To my surprise I have discovered that some feminists regard 'fellowship' as sexist, for they believe it to be a masculine term and would prefer to speak of 'friendship group'. I am not convinced. Etymologically 'fellowship' is not a male term. Furthermore, there is a greater depth to the term 'fellowship'. In the words of 1 John 1:3: 'We declare to you what we have seen and heard so that you may also have fellowship with us; and truly our fellowship is with the Father and with his Son Jesus Christ'.[1] However, if the term 'fellowship' is for some compromised by gender influence, then perhaps we need just to speak of 'small groups'.

What is not contested is that we live in a world where, in the words of Mother Teresa, many are 'hungry for love, for understanding love, which is ... the only answer to loneliness and great poverty ... People are suffering from terrible loneliness, terrible despair, terrible hatred, feeling unwanted, feeling helpless, feeling hopeless. They have forgotten how to smile, they have forgotten the beauty of the human touch. They are forgetting what is human love. They need someone who will understand and respect them.'[2]

Furthermore, loneliness is not just found in the world beyond

---

[1] See Stephen Smalley, *1, 2, 3 John* (Word, Waco, Texas 1984) 12: 'Christian fellowship is not the sentimental and superficial attachment of a random collection of individuals, but the profoundly mutual relationship of those who remain "in Christ" and therefore belong to each other (see 3:23-24). Just how deep this fellowship can be is indicated by the phrase "to *have* fellowship"; this expresses not just the fact, but also the conscious enjoyment, of fellowship in Jesus Christ.'

[2] I cannot now find the source of this quotation.

the church. Many church people today are also crying out to be affirmed, valued, and loved. Yet nobody can be affirmed, valued, or loved within a crowd. According to Keith Miller, 'Our churches are filled with people who outwardly look contented and at peace, but inwardly are crying out for someone to love them just as they are – confused, frustrated, often frightened, guilty, and often unable to communicate even within their own families. But the other people in the church look so happy and contented that one seldom has the courage to admit his own deep needs before such a self-sufficient group as the average church meeting appears to be.'[3]

Relationships in many a church can be likened to a game of billiards or snooker, where balls fly in all directions, knocking into one another, but never relating to one another. After a morning service people ask one another: 'And how are you this morning?' 'Fine, thank you' is the reply – and off they walk without revealing that inwardly they are far from fine – their personal world is in chaos; their job is perhaps on the line; their son is going off the rails; their ageing parent is causing them concern. But they are afraid to be honest with one another in case people look down upon them. 'Fancy, you losing your job – clearly you can't be all that good at your job.' 'Fancy, your son is going off the rails – clearly you can't have done all that good a job as a parent.' 'Fancy, your mother or father is causing you concern – clearly you are not facing up to your responsibilities as a son or daughter.' They are afraid to be honest, in case people look down upon them – they are afraid, because they are insecure. They are insecure in the sense that they are not sure of the other's love. They wonder: 'Will they love me, warts and all?'.

Small groups, first and foremost, are where we can be real with one another; and are places where love can be meaningfully given and meaningfully expressed. Admittedly, this is not easy. It is not easy being honest and open with others, for to do so people must be prepared to make themselves vulnerable. But once one person in a small group is prepared to be real, often others are prepared to be real too. In the words of the American writer Scott Peck:

---

[3] Keith Miller, *The Taste of New Wine* (Word, Hemel Hempstead, 1965) quoted by Howard Snyder, *New Wineskins* (Marshall, Morgan and Scott, London, 1977), 80.

Vulnerability in community snowballs. Once its members become vulnerable and find themselves being valued and appreciated, they become more and more vulnerable, the walls come tumbling down. And as they tumble, as the love and acceptance escalate, as the mutual intimacy multiplies, true healing and converting begins. Old wounds are healed, old resentments forgiven, old resistances overcome. Fear is replaced by hope.[4]

Although there can be drawbacks to small groups – without the right leadership and the right material it is possible for them to become places where people share mutual ignorance or mutual prejudice – in my experience they are the best way in which meaningful fellowship can be shared. Indeed, without such sharing, I would go so far as to say that church life is a sham.

---

[4] Scott Peck, *The Different Drum: Community Making & Peace* (Simon & Schuster, New York 1985).

LARGE IS ALSO BEAUTIFUL

Larger churches are not 'better' than smaller churches, they are simply different. I believe that there is a place for both small and larger churches. Unfortunately in Britain there is a negative mindset on the part of many ministers of smaller churches toward larger churches. Their mantra is 'small is beautiful'.[1] They fail to see that 'large' can be 'beautiful' too. Tim Chester and Steve Timmis, for instance, on the basis of Jesus' likening his disciples to a 'little flock' (Luke 12:32) argued that 'at the heart of Jesus' future… are small unassuming churches'; and that only a small church can be 'the church of the cross'.[2] But as one colleague said to me: 'If we take the words of Jesus seriously when he said that he would build his church, we would never be satisfied with "small" church'. Another critic argued that churches with more than 200 members 'do not take mission seriously' and are complacent and inward-looking; they 'encourage attendance on the "consumer pattern"', and 'those who attend such churches are in danger of being "takers" rather than givers'.[3]

I find such criticisms depressing. As one whose first church grew to 300 committed members (with many others in attendance too) and whose second church grew to 400 committed members (again with many others in attendance) I know these criticisms are not true. Furthermore, my experience of my first church, which had a membership of 83 when I arrived, is not that the church became less committed when it had 300 members.

---

[1] See E. F. Schumacher, *Small is Beautiful: Economics As If People Mattered* (1978).
[2] Tim Chester and Steve Timmis, *Total Church: A radical reshaping around gospel and community* (IVP, Nottingham, 2007), 194.
[3] Roy Dorey, 'Minorities and Honeypots', *Baptist Ministers Journal*, 301 (Jan/Feb 2009), 8-10.

As a result of having preached in many churches on a 'one-off' basis, I know from first hand experience that some smaller churches can lack vision and can define success in terms of keeping the doors of the church open for another year. Again, I know that people who come to a larger church as a result of surfing the web are not to be condemned as 'consumers', for often they search the web to meet a particular need.

Instead of criticising one another, greater respect and understanding are called for. The fact that churches are different in size does not mean that one is 'better' than another. So why then do larger churches attract people?

1. Larger churches give a warm welcome. Time and again people visiting larger churches comment on the warmth of the greeting they receive. At first sight this might seem strange. One might think that visitors in a larger church would get lost in the crowd and would not receive much of a welcome, whereas in a smaller church visitors would be immediately noticeable and would therefore feel much more welcome. The truth is that most larger churches go to great efforts to ensure that visitors are made welcome. Larger churches tend to have welcome teams, who are keen to learn the names of newcomers, and ready to show people to their seats and in the process introduce them to others in the church. Some larger churches even give gifts to newcomers. There is a 'professionalism' behind the welcome not always found in a smaller church. This is not to say that small churches do not welcome others, but simply that larger churches tend to ensure there always is a welcome.

2. Larger churches can provide anonymity for people seeking a haven. The experience of larger churches is that they often attract Christians who have been hurt or bruised as a result of church 'fights'. Larger churches also tend to attract people who have been 'burnt out' and are exhausted from having to take on too much responsibility in a smaller church. Larger churches provide space for people to recover from bad experiences in smaller churches. Being a 'passenger' can be part of a healing process. Please note:

I am not saying that it is just smaller churches which wound people. Church fights can also take place in larger churches.

3. Larger churches are more seeker-friendly, in the sense that non-Christians do not feel as conspicuous. It is much more difficult for a non-Christian to try out a small church. Please note: I am not saying that large crowds are a necessity for effective evangelism. Some larger churches run Alpha courses with fewer people on the course compared to those who might attend the average sized 'small' church: however, what helps in that in a larger church most people at Alpha are not church people.

4. Larger churches tend to be positive places. People in larger churches often feel good about their church, their minister(s), and their activities. As a result of their good experience of church, they are happy to tell their friends about their church. People look forward to coming to church – church is a great place to be. Not surprisingly people are attracted to them. Please note: I am not saying that small churches by contrast are negative places. However, sometimes smaller churches can be marked by a sense of tiredness, routine, and even failure. It can be tough being a member of a smaller church.

5. The worship and preaching of larger churches is attractive, not only because of the quality of the 'performance', but also their vibrancy of spirit. In an age when people are media-savvy, this is important. It is easier for worship in the larger church to become a 'celebration'. Please note: I am not saying that there are no vibrant small churches. Nor am I saying that the Spirit is only present when crowds flock to worship. Isaiah's encounter with God in his Temple (Isaiah 6) was probably a very personal and individual experience.

6. Larger churches offer something for everybody. Small churches are often unable to run a full programme for children and young people; they are also unlikely to have

activities for young singles.[4] Large churches are also able to offer a range of worship styles. All this is attractive to many.

I recognise that not everybody is attracted to a larger church. Many prefer the intimacy of a smaller church; they like the sense of 'family' which comes from everybody knowing one another. Difficulties, however, arise for the smaller church when it seeks to be a 'large church writ small'. Instead of smaller churches seeking to be 'all things to all people' (see 1 Cor 9:22), they probably need to do just one or two things well. In 'shopping' terms, there is a place for the small 'boutique' as well as for the larger 'supermarket'.

Small can be 'beautiful' – but so too can large churches be beautiful!

---

[4] John Drane, *After McDonaldization: Mission, ministry and Christian discipleship in an age of uncertainty* (Darton, Longman and Todd, London, 2008), 94: 'Single people ... typically find a large church can offer the chance to meet others who are single, without feeling pressurised to conform to stereotypes based on a norm of married life'

CHURCH BUILDINGS MATTER

'Church buildings – a monumental waste of time'. This was the title of a blog, which went on to say:

> It is sad to see so much time, money, effort, energy and focus being spent on church buildings, their upkeep and expansion, buildings that not only don't even need to exist, but shouldn't exist. Millions of dollars are often wasted on just one of the countless thousands upon thousands of church buildings that litter the landscape, money that could have been used to help transform a local community by showing the love of God in real action to people who are in need. But no, we can't have that! We need to build endless meeting places for our comfort and convenience. Strange, but not one time, not in one single place in all of the Bible do we ever see Christians building a church building, let alone for their comfort and convenience.[1]

Howard Snyder also believed church buildings to be largely superfluous. He argued that they are a witness to 'the immobility, inflexibility, lack of fellowship, pride, and class divisions in the modern church'.[2]

Rick Warren of Saddleback fame has also been critical of church buildings:

> Church buildings can be a major barrier to exponential growth. Massive building programs are often a waste of money. History has proven over and over that future generations never fill the cavernous temples of previous generation .... God blesses anointed people, not buildings ...

---

[1]'Church buildings – a monumental waste of time', ChristiansFree.com (no date found).
[2] Howard Snyder, *New Wineskins*, 65.

We also need to remember that the period of fastest growth for Christianity was during the first 300 years – when there were no church buildings at all. And today most of the rapidly exploding church-planting movements around the world are multiplying without having physical church buildings. They've learned to spread out! Buildings should be tools for ministry, not monuments … Churches should focus on building people, not building buildings … I am absolutely opposed to building ANY size of facility that will only be used once or twice a week. It is poor stewardship of God's money to build a facility just because the pastor wants to speak to everyone at one time … If you must build, I urge you to at least consider making it a multi-purpose facility.'[3]

There is truth in these criticisms. Buildings are not essential to the being of the church. The church is people, not buildings. The temple at Jerusalem was replaced by the Body of Christ. People therefore come first; buildings are only secondary. But buildings can serve the people of God, not least in providing a base for worship and mission. I believe that buildings can be good investment in mission.

Let me elaborate. It would be true to say that in the first half of my ministry I never gave church buildings much thought. My first church in Altrincham had a building, which needed some attention. We therefore improved the entrance to the building, but there was no need to raise funds for the project: the money needed was limited and so came out of the church budget. It would be true to say that at that stage I was critical of ministers who spent time and money on redeveloping their church buildings, and felt (unjustly as I now believe) that such ministers, desperate to make their mark, were probably compensating for few conversions by building bigger and better barns.

However, in the second half of my ministry my attitude radically changed. I found myself leading a church whose Edwardian building spoke of a God who belonged to the past. Its solid oak front doors open only a few hours on a Sunday, held little appeal and enticed nobody but the already committed to enter. Inside

---

[3] Rick Warren, 'Does your church really need a bigger building?', 6 February 2015: pastors.com/big-buildings.

the dark and depressing 'sanctuary' with its uncomfortable pews and a massive high pulpit made contemporary worship well-nigh impossible. The buildings were working against the mission of the church. I realised that something had to be done. In the words of Kenneth White, 'If the church is to hold its own... compared with, say well-appointed modern pubs, it has to appeal to people. We know that we have the Word of Life – but folk outside don't. The miracle is that so many people are converted today, despite us and our premises. How many more wait to be attracted?'.[4] Just as our local cinema had to knock down its old 'flea pit' and build a new complex to attract people back to the cinema, so we needed to upgrade our facilities and attract a new church-going public. To cut a long story short, instead of giving the place a lick of paint, we gutted the buildings and eventually ended up with a brand-new mission facility which cost us £2 million. It was an enormous sum of money, but to my amazement the process of having to raise the money became the means of spiritual renewal. What had tended to be an inward-looking church became an outward looking church; what had been a sometime dysfunctional church became a warm loving fellowship. The church became a seven-day-a-week centre for holistic mission, serving the community, winning people for Jesus Christ.

In the process of the re-building, when we had to worship on a Sunday in the Chelmsford County High School for Girls, I discovered the many drawbacks of a church not having a building of its own. Here I have in mind not how time demanding it was to set up the school hall for the weekly Sunday services, but also how difficult it was to engage in serving the community. As I wrote in a subsequent article:

> Some critics have been more radical and questioned whether we need a building at all. After all, Christians didn't have buildings until around 200 AD. Our experience of having worshipped in a school for some 19 months is that there are real disadvantages in renting other people's premises. Setting-up for services was enormously time-demanding. And a school hall is not the most uplifting of environments in

---

[4] Kenneth White, *The Attractive Church* (Grove, Bramcote, Nottinghamshire, 1979), 22.

which to worship God. And as for the all the other activities we ran during the week, it was a nightmare re-locating our two mental-health clubs, our child-contact centre, and all the other activities one might expect of a busy church. It is difficult to engage in holistic mission without a building. Home groups have a role to play, not least in the area of enhancing and deepening fellowship, but they have their limitations when it comes to worship, evangelism and social service. Furthermore, the life-expectancy of churches which do not have buildings of their own tends to be much shorter than those which do invest in bricks and mortar. It is actually good stewardship to invest in church buildings.[5]

Chelmsford Cathedral, where I now worship is a beautiful building, which uplifts the soul and is a great aid to the worship of God. However, it is also a highly flexible space which is used for a wide range of activities seven days a week. But for the Cathedral to be engaged more effectively in holistic mission, it really needs more purpose-built space. If I were the Dean, I would encourage the Cathedral community to launch out into a major building project! For, as I have discovered from my own experience, buildings can make an enormous difference – buildings do matter!

[5] Paul Beasley-Murray, 'Buildings are a good investment in mission', *Baptist Times*, 17 February 2005.

CITY AND TOWN-CENTRE CHURCHES
HAVE A SPECIAL ROLE TO PLAY

My first church was not a city or town-centre church. Like most churches, we were a neighbourhood church. Many people walked to church, while those who came by car could find a parking place relatively easily.

My second church was a town-centre church. Although not in the High Street, we were opposite the main library, near the station, and on the route between the bus station and the market. People were always passing the church. Few people walked to church, and free car parking became increasingly difficult. We had no local neighbourhood to which to minister. (Since I retired, the centre of Chelmsford has been redeveloped and there are increasing numbers of people living in city centre flats designed primarily for commuters.) To the 'chagrin' of the two smaller 'neighbourhood' Baptist churches in town, many people who attended our church passed them on their way to worship with us. They preferred to be part of a large church, with a wider range of activities than any small church could offer.

To my surprise, even though nobody lived around the church, we still were able to offer many of the facilities of a neighbourhood church. We ran well-supported activities for every age group, and, despite the challenge of parking, people would drive in midweek to take advantage of what we had to offer. However, we were clear that unlike neighbourhood churches we had a special role to play in our town. As we said in our 'development plan': 'At a time when most city-centre churches are in decline, our vision is to be a vibrant seven-day-a-week city-centre church, witnessing in word and deed to the love of Jesus. We want to be strong, not for the sake of growth, but for the sake of making a greater impact on our city for Christ: certainly, if we are to expand our service to the community then we will need more people.'

We took seriously Jeremiah's message to the Jewish exiles in Babylon: 'Seek the welfare of the city … and pray to the Lord on its behalf' (Jer. 29:7). We saw the whole town as our 'parish'. At one stage we considered the option of moving out of the centre and building a new church on the edge of town. We could then have had a church with lots of parking, which would probably have enabled us to attract more people on a Sunday. However, we also wanted to serve the community at large. Believing that God had called us to be a town-centre church, we resolved to remain where we were and went on to redevelop the buildings at a cost of £2 million so that we might have a mission facility fit for the twenty-first century.

In addition to all the activities any neighbourhood church might have, we expressed our commitment to the town in ways which would have not been possible if we had been on the edge of town. We ran two mental health clubs, a weekly child contact centre for broken families, a resource centre for Africans seeking a decent job, and a five-day-a-week café which attracted not just shoppers but also the lonely. In addition, we allowed the community to rent out space for special events: at one point we reckoned that from those bookings we were serving 1000+ people a week.

I am conscious that there was more we could have done as a town-centre church. In our development plan we spoke of our desire 'to be a critical friend of the City and County Councils, with a view to supporting social justice in our community', but we never managed to implement that goal. We always seemed to have other priorities. On reflection perhaps this is something best done together with other town-centre churches. On the other hand, we were heavily involved with other churches in the local street pastors' scheme. We also were supportive of a local project for homeless single adults, which had been founded by the churches of the town.[1]

I have spoken of my second church as both a 'town' centre and

---

[1] We also developed a policy for caring for the homeless: see Paul Beasley-Murray & Martin Hills, 'A draft policy for the treatment and care of the homeless', *Ministry Today* 39 (Spring 2007), 43-45.

a 'city' centre church. This is because technically we were both. However, Chelmsford, with a population of around 100,000 is not a major city like London or Birmingham. Although there is a foodbank, 'multiple deprivation', which tends to be distinctive of inner cities, is not present.

I find it interesting to compare Chelmsford Cathedral, which also happens to be the parish church of the city centre, with my former Baptist church less than 500 yards away. The Cathedral very much sees itself as a 'civic' church. The Dean, for instance, prefers to be called the Dean of Chelmsford, rather than the Dean of Chelmsford Cathedral – a title which as a Nonconformist I find demeans the other ministers in the town. It is, however, true that the Cathedral is the venue for a wide variety of civic services. Furthermore, the Cathedral clergy have good relationships with figures such as the Lord Lieutenant and the High Sheriff, the local judges and politicians, the 'chain gang' consisting of the mayors and mayor-equivalents of Essex, and key figures in the City and County Councils. Inevitably as part of an 'established' church the Cathedral has immediate access to 'the powers that be' – an access which most other churches do not have. It so happens that over the years I was able to gain access to 'the movers and shakers' of the city, primarily through being married to the county's senior coroner. However, in terms of actual community service – 'boots on the ground' – the Cathedral's engagement is limited. In making this comment I am not seeking to be critical of the Cathedral. Indeed, I am challenged by the way in which the Cathedral and Anglican churches in general are often much more 'outward facing' than Baptists with their emphasis on the 'gathered' church. What I do find difficult is when Anglicans claim to be the 'Church' without reference to the other denominations and 'streams' which together make up the Church of Christ in England. When it comes to mission and ministry in the cities and towns of England, what is needed is a more collaborate style of ministry, where churches, groups and agencies who share Kingdom values work together in partnership.

LEADERS MAKE THINGS HAPPEN

Andrew Le Peau, in *Paths of Leadership*, quoted a number of great leaders of the past. Harry Truman, for instance, once said, 'A leader is a person who has the ability to get others to do what they don't want to do, and to like it'. Mahatma Gandhi identified tenacity as the key element: 'To put up with misrepresentation and to stick to one's guns come what may – this is the essence of leadership.' Hannibal, as he contemplated crossing the Alps, typified this attitude: 'I will find a way or make one.' Napoleon believed a leader is 'a dealer in hope'; while the ancient Chinese philosopher, Lao-tse, said, 'A leader is best when people barely know he exists.' Andrew Le Peau himself defined leadership as 'any influence any person has on an individual or group to meet its needs or goals for the glory of God.'[1]

Which is right? Which is wrong? All are right! All are fascinating insights into leadership. All are reminders that there is no one style of leadership. All have something to say to ministers involved in Christian leadership.

I like the definition: 'Leaders make things happen.' The challenge then arises to all in church leadership: 'What things are we making happen?' Another helpful definition is: 'Leaders make a difference.' Similarly, the question then arises to all in church leadership: 'What difference are we making?'

What are the qualities needed for leaders to make things happen or to make a difference? According to Montgomery, whose leadership was key to turning around the fortunes of the British Army in North Africa during the Second World War, leadership is 'the capacity to rally men and women to a common purpose,

---

[1] Andrew Le Peau, *Paths of Leadership* (Scripture Union, London, 1984), 9-10.

and the character which inspires confidence'. 'A leader,' he said, 'must exercise an effective influence, and the degree to which he can do this will depend of the personality of the man [sic] – the *incandescence* of which he is capable, the flame which burns within him, the magnetism which will draw the hearts of men toward him.'[2] Much as I agree with the thrust of this definition, it can be misleading, for it can suggest that leadership always demands 'heroic' character, whereas the reality is that vision and passion can also be expressed by 'quieter' forms of leadership.[3]

I discovered a more helpful statement of qualities necessary for leadership in a visit I made to the Auckland Maritime Museum, where there is an exhibition featuring the work of Sir Peter Blake, the man behind New Zealand's successful America's Cup bid. Following his death, a Blake medal is issued every year for outstanding leadership which displays the following qualities:

> *Determination and the will to succeed*
> *Belief in achieving extraordinary things*
> *Willingness to learn*
> *Desire for constant improvement*
> *Trusting and empowering team-mates*
> *The initiative to pursue an idea*
> *Ability to have fun*

I have come to believe that leadership is the key pastoral task. At a time when the church in the West is facing massive decline, leadership is indispensable, for without leadership churches lose direction and ultimately die. Over the years I have frequently quoted the words of Lloyd Perry written within a North American context: 'There are three requirements for a good programme within the church. The first is leadership, the second is leadership, and the third is leadership. A lack of leadership may be part of the reason that in a typical year, an average of at least eight protestant congregations disappear every day... Churches need more leaders, not more members.'[4] This is true not just of churches in America,

---

[2] Bernard Montgomery, *The Art of Leadership* (Collins, London, 1961; reprinted 2009).
[3] See Brian Harris, *The Tortoise Usually Wins: Biblical Reflections on Quiet Leadership for Reluctant Leaders* (Paternoster, Milton Keynes, 2013).
[4] Lloyd Perry, *Getting the Church on Target* (Moody Press, Chicago, 1977), 3.

but of churches in many other parts of the world too. Ministers have a key leadership role to play in making things happen, in making the difference. They are the primary catalyst for growth. In a survey of 350 English Baptist churches, Alan Wilkinson and I established that it was not preaching or pastoral care which helped a church to grow, but leadership, vision, and 'possibility thinking'[5]

Of course, not all forms of leadership are acceptable. 'Some misleaders', wrote Al Gini and Ronald Green, 'are simply pathetic egocentric scoundrels or selfishly adolescent narcissists, full of bluster and pomposity, who enjoy a bright moment and then are quickly and happily forgotten or dismissed.' They instanced such figures as Benito Mussolini, the strutting peacock and Italian dictator; King Farouk, the corpulent playboy and pharaoh of Egypt; Joseph McCarthy, the Wisconsin senator and self-styled inquisitioner of all things communist; and Donald J. Trump, described then as a television personality and an outrageous pompadour. 'Other misleaders,' they wrote, 'are pathological liars, completely sociopathic in their interactions with others and utterly Machiavellian in their use of power.'[6] They instanced such villains as Joseph Stalin, who caused the death of at least 20 million of his own people; Pol Pot of the Khmer Rouge, who created the 'killing fields' of Cambodia; and Robert Mugabe, who ended up destroying the agriculture, financial and social structure of one of the richest nations in Africa.

'Misleaders' are found not only in the world beyond the church, but in the church itself. In churches large and small leaders abuse their power. Any form of Christian leadership needs to go hand-in-hand with character that reflects the servant-heart of Jesus. However, the fact that there are forms of unacceptable leadership does not rule out the need for leadership within the church. If today's churches are to face up today to the challenges offered by contemporary culture, then they desperately need leaders who will think through those challenges and who will enable their churches to make the necessary changes to their life in order to fulfil the Great Commission.

---

[5] Paul Beasley-Murray and Alan Wilkinson, *Turning the Tide*, 35, 36.
[6] Gini and Green, *10 Virtues of Outstanding Leaders*, 18, 19.

TEAMS EMPOWER GOD'S PEOPLE

Throughout my ministry I have been in the business of creating teams, for teams are a way of empowering God's people for mission and ministry. Ministers are not to monopolise ministry, but to multiply ministry. To quote Andrew Le Peau: 'Organisations that are built on the preaching, teaching, thinking, entertaining, fund-raising charisma of one person – of which there are many in Christendom – are built contrary to Scripture. These are not bodies. These are grotesque mutations.'[1]

There is no place for the 'one-man band', in which a single minister plays all the instruments. Rather, the minister's role is like the conductor of an orchestra. 'In an orchestra the task of the conductor is to get all the members functioning together and playing in harmony. It is not his [sic] job to dash around the seats playing all the instruments himself [sic] one after another.'[2] Alternatively, the minister has been likened to a rowing coach, whose task is to get every member pulling their weight, and to train them as a crew to row effectively. Or even better, ministers should follow Tom Cadnam's advice and model themselves on rugby captains:

> In New Zealand we have two favourite sports, cricket in the summer and rugby football in the winter. In cricket, one man can virtually win the day. If he scores many runs when batting and bowls out several of the opposition when fielding, it is possible for other team members to fail or stand around him and watch him produce results. With rugby this seldom if ever happens. For the whole game, the whole team is on the field, including the captain. He must lead and inspire

---

[1] Andrew T. Le Peau, *Paths of Leadership* (British Edition: Scripture Union, London, 1984), 60.
[2] Michael Griffiths, *Cinderella with Amnesia* (IVP, London, 1975), 59.

but without a team effort, it is virtually impossible for one
man to win the game. The image Paul uses of the ministry
is more akin to that of a rugby captain than that of a cricket
captain. Ministers are encouragers of the team, all of whom
are engaged in mission. At no point of the game can they be
spectators. Sadly the pattern we have developed is that of the
minister as 'super-player', who, by his [sic] skill and prowess,
keeps the team going while most of the players spend their
time in the pavilion (pews) hoping that he [sic] will not let
them down.[3]

Most churches have one basic leadership team. The name that is
given to this team varies: some churches talk of the board or the
oversight, others of the elders or the deacons, while yet others of
the PCC. Just as in the New Testament there was no one pattern
for a leadership team, neither does there have to be one pattern
today.

Working together in a team has great advantages.

- Leaders are able to complement one another, for no
  one has all the gifts necessary for an all-round ministry.
  Members of a leadership team can build up one another's
  strengths and compensate for one another's weaknesses
- Leaders are able to encourage one another. Leadership can
  be a lonely business, but where leadership is shared, there
  support can be derived. Members of a leadership team can
  identify one another's gifts and encourage each other to
  develop and use them.
- Leaders are able to be accountable to one another. It is
  not good for either the individual or the church if a leader
  is not in a position to receive correction when things go
  wrong. Members of a leadership team should be able to
  speak the truth in love to one another (see Eph. 4:15), and
  so learn from failure and be the stronger for the future.

A leadership team need not be the only team in the church. In both
my churches I introduced 'task' teams. In Altrincham we had teams

---

[3] Tom Cadman, 'How I practise my ministry', *Baptist World Alliance Commission on Pastoral Leadership*
(Maclean, Virginia, 1982).

responsible for social action, evangelism, nurture, development of individuals, and pastoral care; in Chelmsford we created even more task teams, each taking responsibility for particular areas of the church's mission and ministry, and in this way freed the leadership team to focus on the bigger picture of the role God would have the church play.

In larger churches there may be a staff team, consisting perhaps not just of ordained ministers but of others who together form a 'ministry team'. The task of the 'team leader' is to weld the team together. Alas, all too often relationships can break down. It has been said that 'It is rare to find one out of four multiple staffs working in love and harmony. Many team members merely tolerate each other. They resemble married couples living together like singles who have no commitment, common goals, or sense of sharing. They simply share the same house.'[4] As a result I developed the following team 'covenant' for our ministry team:

- Mutual care. We will model the kind of relationships that ideally should characterise the life of the church in general. We will love one another, pray for one another, honour one another, care for one another, encourage one another, speak the truth in love to one another, and always forgive one another. We will be there for one another, come hell or high water.

- Communication. We will keep one another informed of what we are doing and of what we are hoping of doing. We will therefore come to our team meetings ready to share.

- Openness. We will be open with one another. There may be times when the ministers will not be free to be open with the rest of the team, however, there is no place for ministers to keep secrets from one another. Confidentiality does not necessarily mean that we cannot share information with one another.

- Honesty. In our thoughts and our feelings we will be honest with one another. If something has upset us, then we will surface it, recognising that 'Today's niggle could

---

[4] Harold J. Westing, *Church Staff Handbook: How to build an effective ministry team* (Kregel, Grand Rapids, Michigan, 2nd edition, 1997), 13.

be tomorrow's resentment, and next week's breakdown'.

- Loyalty. Outside our team meeting, we will always stand up for one another. While none of us is perfect, and there will be times when we make a mess of things, we will resist the temptation of criticising one another to other members. The place for criticism is either one-to-one or in the team meeting.
- Positivity. In our relationships with one another, and with the rest of the church, we will always exude a positive spirit. We will shun negative talking and thinking. We will instead affirm one another and will speak well of one another.
- Excellence: We will never be satisfied with the second-best. In our desire for excellence we will foster a healthy dissatisfaction with the way things are and will always strive for better.
- Faith: We will strengthen one another's hope and faith in God, and we will foster each other's passion for Christ. We will be bold in the way we develop our various ministries; and where there are failures, we will help one another to learn and then to use the failure as a stepping board for fresh advances.

Good leaders are in the business of creating and maintaining teams, for teams are a key way of empowering God's people for service. But for this to happen ministers need to be good team players themselves – happy to share ministry with others, happy to allow others to take initiatives, and happy to lead but not to control.

CONSTANT CHANGE IS HERE TO STAY

I belong to the generation that at school used dipping pens and inkpots. What a difference using a fountain pen made! Then people moved on to 'ball-points' and 'biros'. Interestingly, the fountain pen has now become fashionable again – it is certainly the best kind of instrument with which to write a letter of condolence. I can still remember washing mangles and '78' records. Those were the days when Latin was a central feature on many a school syllabus, and not even scientists or medics could get into Cambridge without having a Latin O level. At Cambridge we all had to wear gowns for lectures, for evening hall, and if we went out of an evening. What is more, in my men-only college the gates were locked at 10 p.m. – special permission from one's tutor was required to stay out later!

Change has become the new normal. In the words of John F. Kennedy, '… change is the law of life. And those who look to the past or present are certain to miss the future.'[1] Moreover, not only has the pace of change accelerated, the types of changes are becoming transformational. Think Apple; think Amazon; think Airbnb; think Uber.

The church has changed too. In many churches hymn-books have gone, organs have gone, choirs have gone, pews have gone, even pulpits have gone. Worship has changed, preaching has changed, even taking up the offering has changed.

According to Thomas Rainer in the past ten years American churches that are doing 'relatively well' have made eight major changes to their church life:[2]

---

[1] John F. Kennedy's address to the Assembly Hall at the Pauluskirche in Franfurt, 25 June 1963.
[2] Seethomrainer.com/2017/eight-major-changes-the past ten years.

- Smaller worship gatherings as distinct from larger worship gatherings; for Millennials like smaller gatherings, therefore multiple services are required.
- Smaller church facilities as distinct from larger church facilities, for leaders are more hesitant to spend funds on largely unused spaces during the week.
- First 'staff' person hired is now a children's minister rather than a worship leader (Millennials are looking for a church that is fun for their children).
- A ministry degree is now optional for church staff members, who often come from within the congregation – in the past staff members were college-trained.
- A new emphasis on congregational singing rather than on the performance of the praise team and band.
- Community focus as distinct from community myopia.
- Small groups are a high priority and no longer an optional extra.
- Church leaders are continuous learners, and no longer 'degree and done'.

I have no idea what changes will take place in British churches, but what I do know is that change is not an option. Churches either change or they die. A few years ago Robin Gill, a British sociologist and theologian, likened British churches today to 'the pelicans in St James's Park' in central London, who he said are, 'Awkward, out of place, angular, with a big mouth but little brain, demanding but inactive.' He went on: 'Churches in Britain need to make urgent choices about structure and direction. If they are to cease being pelicans, they need to be much clearer about how they might be effective in present-day Britain. They need to be more single-minded about growth ... about how they might reach the nine out of ten people in Britain who seldom or never go to church.'[3]

Around the same time William Easum, an American Methodist church consultant, made a similar point, but likened churches to dinosaurs: 'Congregations whose membership has plateaued or is declining have much in common with dinosaurs. Both have

---

[3] Robin Gill, *A Vision for Growth: Why your church doesn't have to be a pelican in the wilderness* (SPCK, London, 1994), 2-3.

great heritages. Both require enormous amounts of food ...
Both became endangered species ... Like the dinosaur they have
a voracious appetite. Much of their time, energy, and money is
spent foraging for food (for themselves), so that little time is left to
feed the unchurched ... Either their pride or their near-sightedness
keeps them from changing the ways they minister to people ...
All around are unchurched, hurting people ... But many refuse to
change their methods and structures to minister to people where
they are in ways they can understand. Like the dinosaur, their necks
are too stiff or their eyes too near-sighted. Clearly God doesn't
care if these congregations survive; but God passionately cares if
they meet the spiritual needs of those God sends their way.'[4]

Unconsciously no doubt, far too many churches exist for
themselves. Feeling happy as they are, they turn their backs on
change, and then wonder why they fail to attract others. It is all
too easy to blame the hardness of people's hearts outside, when in
fact the trouble is caused by the self-centredness of God's people.

Yet it is not enough for a church to change its way of doing
church. It needs to constantly change. Churches – and indeed
leaders – can never afford to sit back on their laurels. We have
never arrived. We are always 'en route' to our goal. What is more,
our tactics constantly need to change if we are to reach the goal.
In this regard churches can be likened to sailing ships, which need
to tack first in one direction and then in another direction if they
are to catch the wind of the Spirit. This means that it is not enough
for ministers to make changes brought into church life by their
predecessors; they in turn need to be willing to make changes to
things they themselves initiated!

Making changes to church life is a challenging business.
Change is a process which takes time. As a friend once said,
sudden change 'is a bit like having a baby without being pregnant
for nine months. The leaders have spent many hours and days
in discussion, in the gestation of the idea. Then the "baby" is
suddenly presented to the church which perhaps has just forty-
five minutes to make up its mind! No wonder there are so many

---

[4] William Easum, *Dancing with Dinosaurs: Ministry in a Hostile and Hurting World* (Abingdon, Nashville,
1993), 14-15.

unhappy births.' The congregation must share in the pregnancy if it is to be a healthy baby.[5]

If a major change is to be successfully introduced, plenty of time must be given for the church to absorb its implications. As I have discovered, if leaders are to take the church as a whole with them, they must pay careful attention to the various rates of adoption as also to the various categories of adopters. These rates and categories have been classified as follows:

1. Some 2.5% of the church are *'Innovators'*, who are enthusiastic about change and promote its introduction to others.

2. A further 13.5% are *'Early Adopters'*, who are quick to accept the change, and are then happy to promote its introduction.

3. A further 34% form the *'Early Majority'*. Many initially had reservations, but have now been persuaded and now persuade others.

4. A further 34%, the *'Late Majority'*, were initially resistant to the change, but have been gradually won over.

5. The final 16% are the *'Laggards'* who now accept the change grudgingly. The dissidents remain in this group even after the change has become tradition![6]

Obviously there is a good deal of generalisation here. However, there are two key points. First there are always 'dissidents' who will never be won around – and they should never be allowed to hold a church to ransom. Secondly, if a church is not to be split unnecessarily leaders need to ensure that major decisions are not taken by the church until the *'Late Majority'* has come on board. This does not guarantee unanimity: there will always be some die-hard *'Laggards'*. However, without the *'Late Majority'* a church risks literally being split in two.

Clearly there is no Scriptural foundation to such an analysis. However, not to pay attention to such insights is to run the risk

---

[5] Nick Mercer, 'Coping with Change', *The Fraternal* 234 (April 1991), 5.
[6] Everett C. Rogers with F. Floyd Shoemaker, *Communication of Innovations* (Free Press, 2nd edition, 1971) 182.

of being what Paul describes as 'children in your thinking' (1 Cor. 14:20). The fact is that most people, even Christian people, initially resist change. Change, however, is not an option. Wise ministers will not just welcome change, they will also ensure they become change-masters who know how to handle the process of change.

WITHOUT A PLAN VISION
IS ONLY WISHFUL THINKING

'Where there is no vision, the people perish' declared Proverbs 29:18 in The Authorised Version of the Bible, and how true that is![1] Vision is vital – not least in church life. George Carey, a former Archbishop of Canterbury wrote: 'I discovered a common malaise in churches that were in advance stages of ecclesiastical terminal illness – lack of vision. Unless the minister and at least some of the people have a spiritual vision which sees beyond the difficulties of the human situation, everything will seem hopeless. Vision thus becomes the driving force of prayer and the wheels of change are set in motion. It is important also for this vision to be shared with others, so that it may gently permeate the life of the church, creating expectancy and awareness of what is possible.'[2]

Vision, if it is to be more than wishful thinking, needs to be specific. I have found the following list of 'ten characteristics of a good vision' to be most helpful:[3]

1. A vision is related to mission but different. All congregations have the same mission, which is to fulfil our Lord's Great Commission. Vision is insight into how a particular congregation will carry out its mission in its context in the next five to ten years.

2. A vision is unique. Each vision, like a fingerprint, fits the individual congregation that has adopted a vision of how

---

[1] The precise translation of this verse is disputed. J. G. Janzen pointed out 'the conviction in Prov. 29:18a semantically parallels that in Prov. 11:14a, 'Where there is no guidance, a people falls'. However, the guidance in question relates more to God's revelation as expressed in the Torah. See Bruce K. Waltke, *The Book of Proverbs: Chapters 15-31* (Eerdmans, Grand Rapids, 2005), 445-447.
[2] I cannot find the precise source of this quotation.
[3] This is a slight adaptation of a list produced by Paul Borden, which in turn was an adaptation of a list produced by Lovett Weems, *Church Leadership* (Abingdon Press, Nashville, 1993).

God will work in its situation. The vision not only reflects the contextual surroundings of the congregation but the personality and giftedness of the congregation.

3. A vision focuses on the future. While visions honour the past and what God has done to bring a congregation to the present, they focus on a preferred future for each congregation. It is the view of the future that changes the present life of the congregation in order to achieve the preferred future stated in the vision.

4. A vision is for others. The focus of a vision is what it will do for others who are not a part of the group stating the vision. A good vision is quite unselfish in its intent. It places as primary the needs of people not currently being served by the congregation.

5. A vision is realistic. All good visions stretch the imaginations of people, yet they are realistic enough to be achieved if God intervenes. Good visions are not statements of presumption; instead, they are statements of faith.

6. A vision is lofty. Good visions inspire people to high standards and targets not easily achieved. The lofty statements force congregations to be clear about their values while forcing them to choose which values they will honour and implement and which ones they will ignore.

7. A vision is inviting. Passive 'ho-hum' visions do not produce passion, commitment to service and the giving of resources. Visions helps people see how the future can be better and how they can, with God's help, make that happen. Good leaders have the ability to help people see what their good deeds will produce and how corporately the group can achieve so much more than what individuals alone can make happen.

8. Vision is a group vision. All visions are shared by the group. They ring true for a majority of the people.

9. A vision is good news and bad news. It is good news in that it is a promise of a better future. It is bad news because it provides judgment on the past and the present. Therefore a vision always gets mixed reviews.

10. A vision is a sign of hope. Faith, hope, and love are crucial to God's congregations. It is vision that provides a congregation with hope. Vision gives the leader hope and it gives followers hope of what God will do through them.

Yet even a well-thought-through vision for the church and its mission is not sufficient. There needs to be plan. A detailed strategy is called for, and then goals need to be set which are smart, measurable, attainable, relevant, and time-based (so-called SMART goals). What is more the strategy and the goals need to be regularly reviewed. There is no sense in devoting time and energy to creating detailed strategies and goals, and then failing to implement them. I shall never forget Bill Tanner, a former Executive Director of the Southern Baptist Home Mission Board, saying: 'God is going to hold us accountable for the stewardship of our vision'. If God gives his leaders a vision, then he expects them to be serious in implementing the vision. Churches need to know not only the general direction, but also the way that leads in that direction. Strategies and goals need to be formulated.

Yet, some are fearful of creating a strategy and setting goals because they believe it will lead to the Holy Spirit being organised out of the church. This is a false spirituality. God wants us to use our minds as well as to look to him in prayer. God expects us to use our minds in his service: we are not to be 'like horses and mules, which have no understanding, and who must be curbed with bit and bridle' (Ps. 32: 8, 9). God's guidance is often received through the use of our minds. God created us to think – and not to think is to spurn his gifts.

If further Scriptural support is required, then the advice of Prov. 4:26 is helpful: 'Plan carefully what you do and whatever you do will turn out right' (GNB). At the same time we need to recognise that 'we may make our plans, but God has the last word' (Prov. 16:2 GNB). With the help of God's Spirit we may set out a plan, but no plan can be set in stone. Plans need to be 'written in pencil'. Churches need to listen constantly to God and to follow his direction, even if this means changing plans. Yet with that important *caveat*, plans there need to be. For without a plan, vision is only wishful thinking.

LEADERSHIP DEMANDS PASSION

G. W. F. Hegel, the great nineteenth-century German philosopher, said, 'Nothing great in the world has been accomplished without passion'. Passion it is that gives leaders energy and attracts people to follow their lead. Passion enables leaders to influence others. Kent Millard, pastor of an American Methodist mega-church, argued that 'knowing your purpose in ministry is vital, but you also have to have a passion for it or you'll never achieve it. Purpose tells us where we are going, and passion gives us the energy to get there'.[1] 'Purpose', he said, 'comes from the head, passion comes from the heart.'[2]

In the New Testament the term 'passion' (*pathos*) tends to be used of unhealthy sinful sexual urges and therefore has negative connotations.[3] However, in two places both Paul and Peter recognised there is a place for passionate leadership.

1. In Rom. 12:11 Paul wrote: 'Do not lag in zeal, be ardent in spirit, serve the Lord' (NRSV). In other words, if we are to serve the Lord as ministers of the Gospel then we must be on fire for Jesus. The NIV translates the phrase 'be ardent in spirit' as 'keep your spiritual fervour'. John Stott thought the picture Paul had in mind was' not so much of a glowing lamp as of a boiling, bubbling pot' – we are to ensure that we are on the boil spiritually.[4] I prefer the RSV rendering: 'be aglow with the Spirit', with the idea present of keeping the fire of the Holly Spirit burning. If

---

[1] See E. Carver McGriff and M. Kent Millard, *The Passion Driven Congregation* (Abingdon Press, Nashville, 2003), 17.
[2] Carver & Millard, 56.
[3] See Rom. 1:26; 6:12; 7:5; Gal. 5:24; Eph. 2.3; 2 Tim. 2:22; Titus 2:12; 3.3; 1 Pet 4.3
[4] John R. W. Stott, *The Message of Romans* (IVP, Leicester, 1994), 331.

this translation is right, then we have here a reminder that the leader's passion needs to be Spirit-driven.

2. In 1 Pet. 5:2 Peter said to a group of leaders, 'Tend the flock of God ... not for sordid gain, but eagerly' (NRSV). The underlying Greek noun (*prothumos*) is a strong word, which other English versions variously render as 'out of sheer devotion' (REB) or 'from a real desire to serve' (GNB). Wayne Grudem commented that it denotes 'a positive emotional desire'[5] while J. N. D. Kelly noted 'it expresses enthusiasm and devoted zeal'.[6] In other words, Peter is speaking of the necessity of passion. So Kenneth Bailey wrote: 'The shepherds should lead their flocks eagerly (*prothumos*) and passionately. Peter was passionate about many things. He wanted the shepherds of God's new flock to engage in leading his sheep with that same enthusiasm. Passion for the gospel was of utmost importance'.[7]

At one stage I argued that leaders need enthusiasm. 'The word literally means "possession by God". Rightly understood, enthusiasm is a quality generated by the Holy Spirit. Enthusiasts are men and women fired by God's Spirit.'[8] However, I now believe that passion is required instead. For passion is a deeper emotion which is rooted in our very souls.

According to New Zealand church leader Terry Calkin, there are three levels implied in the English word 'passion':

1. 'Deep excitement'. This is the contagion of leadership. This is what makes other people want to follow the leader. This is what makes the leader 'charismatic'. People crave a sense of excitement in their own lives, and when they recognise it in the leader's life, they intuitively want to follow it.

2. 'Deep desire'. This is the element of passion that keeps the leader committed to his objective, even when the 'going gets tough'. Commitment to the task ahead comes

[5] Wayne Grudem, *1 Peter* (IVP, Leicester, 1988), 188.
[6] J. D. D. Kelly, *The Epistles of Peter and of Jude* (A. C. Black, London, 1969), 202.
[7] Kenneth Bailey, *The Good Shepherd* (SPCK, London, 2015), 264.
[8] Paul Beasley-Murray, *Dynamic Leadership* (Marc, Eastbourne, 1990), 185, 186.

directly from the deep desire within the heart of the leader to achieve the common objective. Vision is always tested. It goes with the territory of leadership. If objectives were easy to attain, then leadership would not be required. The deeper the vision is held in the leader's heart, the deeper the commitment will be in the heart of the leader to see it achieved. The task of leadership is to take people through tough times.

3. 'Deep suffering'. We talk about the Passion of Christ, i.e. Christ's suffering upon the cross. Leadership is often a lonely existence. Anyone aspiring to leadership should recognise this. One of the most successful ways of reducing the impact of suffering upon leadership is to build a team around the leader, thus enabling the burdens of leadership to be shared.[9]

In other words, passion is ultimately 'cruciform' in shape. Passion is what we see in the Garden of Gethsemane and on the Cross of Calvary.

In Christian leadership, passion is vital for it is passion which communicates vision. As Steve Moore, President of the American 'Mission Nexus', wrote:

> If vision is 'what you see' as a leader, passion makes what you see important... Most leaders intuitively understand that effective communication calls for both passion and vision. So if passion is limited, a common temptation is to substitute intensity. Followers know the difference. Intensity communicates, 'I really want *you* to believe this'. Passion communicates, '*I* really believe this'. Intensity is marked mostly by *emotion*; passion is marked mostly by *conviction*. Intensity is often packaged with *hype*; passion comes with *authenticity*. Intensity comes across as *superficial*; passion comes across as *natural*. Intensity is communicated by talking *loudly*; passion is communicated by talking *plainly*. There's a place for intensity in leadership, but is no substitute for passion.[10]

---

[9] Terry Calkin and Paul Beasley-Murray, *The Passionate Leader* (Arusha, Tanzania, 2015), 20-21.

[10] Steve Moore, 'Passion and Leadership' growingleaders.com 12 July 2014).

This link between vision and passion is of utmost importance. Vision needs passion – passion needs vision. Vision gives direction to passion – passion motivates vision. The two are inseparably intertwined in an effective leader. Terry Calkin put it this way:

> Vision comes from God. Passion comes from you. When passion and vision mix you have fulfilment. If you have vision without passion you have a daydreamer. If you have passion without vision you have a wheel spinner, all action and nowhere to go. Passion is a strong desire, a drive to see vision come to fulfilment.[11]

Passion is vital to leadership. Without passion our enterprise will falter and eventually fail.

---

[11] Calkin & Beasley-Murray, *The Passionate Leader*, 21.

COMMUNICATE, COMMUNICATE, COMMUNICATE

George Bernard Shaw said, 'The single biggest problem in communication is the illusion that it has taken place'. How right he was: the number of times I've said something to my wife, which she later swears I never mentioned! My true concern, however, is not communication within the marriage, but within the church. How many times do ministers need to highlight some event for the church to truly take on board the message? Once is certainly not enough. Different experts have different ideas for how often a message needs to be communicated. Herbert Krugman believed just three times is enough. He said that three levels of psychological awareness – curiosity, recognition, and decision – could be achieved with just three exposures to a message.[1] However, the most often quoted number is seven. According to the 'Rule of Seven' people need to hear a message seven times before they will consider taking action. Marton Jojoarth said, 'It's not nagging: repetition is effective communication.'[2] This means that if ministers want to communicate well, they should repeat their message seven times, and ideally not just through the same means.

Within a church context there are a number of options. In the first place there is the weekly Sunday 'bulletin' or 'notice sheet', which in many churches is given out not just as a hard copy, but is also emailed out to members and friends. However, not everybody bothers to read the printed message. The message therefore needs

---

[1] Herbert E. Krugman, 'The Impact of Television Advertising: Learning Without Involvement', *Public Opinion Quarterly*, volume 29 (1965), 349.
[2] Martin Jojarth: www.linkedin.com/pulse/its-nagging-repition-effective-communication-marton-jojarth.

to be reinforced. In some 'hi-tech' churches the printed message sheet is accompanied by a fast-moving video presentation shown before or after the service. What is more if the presentation includes some humour, people are inclined to listen (just as airline passengers are more likely to listen to pre-flight safety instructions if they are accompanied by a humorous video).

Nothing can supplant the human voice, particularly if the message-giver is an enthusiast. 'Use print for detail,' wrote John Truscott, but 'speech for effect'.[3] Nonetheless, there is danger in allowing enthusiasts to take over the notice slot. I came to believe that notices were so important that I refused to delegate them to anybody else – drawing the attention of the church to a key event in its life seemed to me to be the task of the senior minister. Precisely because of their importance, I used to prepare carefully what I wanted to say. I gave a good deal of thought as to what needed to be communicated and 'honed' my words accordingly. I also tried not to highlight events which were only of interest to one age-group or section in the church. Notices from the front had to be relevant to the whole church.

Furthermore, such spoken notices had to be given in good time. Now that many people attend church only every second or third week, care needs to be taken that sufficient time is given: just mentioning something a few days before the event will not impact the church as a whole. At least three weeks are needed to begin the build-up to a key event.

Promoting an event cannot be limited to a Sunday. Churches need to put out the message on social media such as Facebook and Twitter, as well as send out short e-mails (long-emails tend not to be read). Then there is texting. According to 'Flocknote', sending a reminder text message the night before an event will double attendance the next day: 'Text messaging (with a 99 per cent open rate, most all of which occurs within the first few minutes) is hands-down the best way to reach the vast majority of your people any time you need to.'[4]

It's not just church events that need to be promoted. The church's vision too needs to be communicated – not just once, but on a regular

---

[3] John Truscott, *A plan for your communications* (Creative Organisation for Christian Ministry, January 2019), 9.
[4] See flocknote.com/blog/8-simpler-ways-improve-your-parish-communication.

basis. Rick Warren developed what he called the Nehemiah principle:

> In Nehemiah's story of rebuilding the wall around Jerusalem, we learn that halfway through the project the people got discouraged and wanted to give up. Like many churches, they lost their sense of purpose and, as a result became overwhelmed with fatigue, frustration, and fear. Nehemiah rallied the people back to work by reorganising the project and recasting the vision. He reminded them of the importance of their work and reassured them that God would help them fulfil his purpose (Neh. 4:6-15) ... Vision and purpose must be restated every 26 days to keep the church moving in the right direction.[5]
>
> Don't assume that a single sermon on the church's purposes will permanently set the direction of our church. Don't suppose that by printing your purposes in the bulletin everyone has learned them, or even read them.[6]

Warren constantly reviews and reiterates the five purposes of his church. I am sure that Warren is right. Communication is vital.

When I was minister of Central Baptist Church, Chelmsford, I too tried to ensure that the vision we had developed was communicated regularly with the church. Three times a year, at the beginning of each 'term', we had a Vision Sunday, when we looked ahead to our vision for the coming term. For the first month or two of each calendar year I would often preach a series of sermons based on our vision and values, rooting the vision and the values within Scripture. At newcomers evenings we spent time explaining the vision and values of the church. We produced fridge magnets, bookmarks, car stickers, and all kinds of leaflets reflecting our vision and our values. As a result everybody knew our mission statement and strap line by heart. In addition, most weeks we had an 'excited spot' at which we reported on what God had been doing that week.[7]

---

[5] Rick Warren, *The Purpose-Driven Church* (Zondervan, Grand Rapids, 1995), 111.

[6] Rick Warren, *Purpose-Driven Church*, 117.

[7] Whenever the Law is summarised within the context of the Eucharist, Anglicans are reminded of the two-fold 'purpose' God has for life: viz. to love him with all our heart, soul, mind and strength; and to love our neighbour as ourselves.

Communication is vital in a church: but do ministers ever check the understanding of their people? Communication needs also to be to two-way. It's not just a matter of transmitting, it is also important to gain confirmation and to make sure that what the church's leaders want to be understood is understood. In a Baptist setting this is the great advantage of the 'church meeting', where members come together to discern the mind of Christ for the life of their church. At the church meeting there is opportunity for leaders to share the vision; and for members to contribute to the vision and in this way own the vision for themselves.

To conclude, 'communication, commnication, communication' is essential not just for the church's well-being, but also for the church's effectiveness in mission.

THE SPIRIT IS NO SUBSTITUTE
FOR HARD WORK

I began my ministry when charismatic renewal was radically changing much church life. At the time there was a temptation in some circles to 'leave everything to the Spirit', as if leaving things to the Spirit effectively discharges us from playing our part and putting our shoulders to the wheel. But as Rob Roxburgh, a Canadian Baptist leading David Pawson's former church in Guildford, wisely said:

> Renewal [and I would extend this to church life in general] is not all a matter of being 'blessed'. It is the hard work of implementing dreams through organisation, structures and strategy through the empowering and enabling of the Holy Spirit ... Most church success stories have as much perspiration as inspiration behind them in the sense that members have worked hard to establish structures and strategies that will fulfil the prompting and vision of the Spirit.[1]

God may give the growth, but we in turn need to 'plant' and 'water' (1 Cor. 3:7, 8). God does not normally choose to work independently of human agents. In this regard, two other passages from the Apostle Paul's writings come to mind.

The first is where Paul compared himself to the other apostles: 'I worked harder than any of them' (1 Cor. 15:10). The underlying Greek verb (*kopiao*) implies real effort. My Greek Lexicon tells me that it means to 'work hard, toil, strive, struggle', and can

---

[1] *Renewal Down to Earth* (Eastbourne, Kingsway, 1987), 135.

also include the sense of 'become weary, tired'.[2] As the Acts of the Apostles shows, Paul was not exaggerating when he said that he had worked harder for the Gospel than any of the other apostles. However, he immediately recognised the folly of such a comparison, for he went on 'although it was not I, but the grace of God that is with me'. Paul knew that at the end of the day everything is down to the grace of God. As Roy Ciampa and Brian Rosner commented: 'Paul does not describe his hard work as a matter of co-operating with God's grace but entirely as an effect of God's grace. What was on display was not a manifestation of Paul's capabilities or efforts, but of the grace of God that was with him.'[3] Similarly, Gordon Fee wrote: 'In Pauline theology, even his labour is a response to grace, it is more properly seen as an effect of grace'.[4]

God's grace does not do away with the need for effort on our part. As David Prior rightly noted: 'The only proper response to grace is total commitment with every fibre of our being. If God's grace does not produce such energetic single-mindedness, there is something seriously lacking in our faith (see Rom. 12:1ff.; Col. 1:27-29)'.[5] Similarly David Johnson said, there is 'a needed delicate balance and insight concerning our own intents, purposes, will and labours with absolute reliance on God's supply of grace for all that we do (see Phil. 2:12-13)'.[6]

The second passage which comes to mind is the text I used to preach on when doing 'deputation' in the churches after having spent two years teaching in Congo/Zaire where I was training future leaders of the African church. Paul in the context of talking about his God-given 'commission' to take the Good News of Jesus to the Gentile world, wrote: 'It is he [Christ] whom we proclaim, warning everyone and teaching everyone in all wisdom, so that we may present everyone mature in Christ. For this I toil and struggle with all the energy that he powerfully inspires within me.' (Col. 1:28). Although I used this text to talk about training people for

---

[2] William Arndt and Wilbur Gingrich, *A Greek Lexicon of the NT and other Early Christian Literature* (Cambridge University Press, 1982).
[3] Roy E. Ciampa & Brian S. Rosner, *The First Letter to the Corinthians* (Apollos, Nottingham, 2010), 752.
[4] Gordon D. Fee, *The First Epistle to the Corinthians* (Eerdmans, Grand Rapids, 1987), 736.
[5] David Prior, *The Message of 1 Corinthians,* (IVP, Leicester, 1985), 262.
[6] David F. Johnson, *1 Corinthians* (IVP, Leicester, 2004), 287.

ministry, these words of Paul are a good summary of what ministry is about. Here too we learn that, 'Public gauges of success, whether large numbers of converts or eloquent speech or architecturally elegant sanctuaries, are not effective measures of a ministry's importance. God calculates success by whether a congregation entrusted to the care of a minister is spiritually fed and fit to the end.'[7]

Paul in seeking to fulfil his calling gave himself totally to the task. In describing the effort involved he used two significant Greek words, which we might paraphrase as, 'I worked myself to the bone, as I experienced the pain and the struggle of ministry.' The main verb is derived from the same Greek verb found in 1 Cor. 15:10 which implies hard labour or 'toil to the point of weariness or exhaustion'.[8] The participle which qualifies the verb comes from a Greek noun (*agon*) from which the English word 'agony' is derived and was used of the struggle involved in seeking to win a race or a fight. Modern English versions translate the phrase as 'I contend strenuously' (NIV), 'I toil and struggle' (GNB), 'I am toiling strenuously' (REB). Ministry for Paul was a demanding and challenging calling which required immense physical, mental and spiritual effort. To put it mildly, it was hard work. Yet, Paul was conscious that at the same time God was working in and through him: 'I toil and struggle with all the energy that he powerfully inspires within me.' Despite his exhausting schedule of work, Paul knew himself to be utterly dependent on God's enabling power. As Ben Witherington noted: 'Paul does not go about his work half-heartedly, hoping vaguely that grace will fill the gaps which he is too lazy to work at himself. Nor, however, does he imagine that it is 'all up to him', so that unless he burns himself out with restless, anxious toil nothing will be achieved.'[9]

---

[7] Robert W. Wall, *Colossians and Philemon* (IVP, Leicester, 1993), 95.

[8] F. F. Bruce, *The Epistles to the Colossians, to Philemon, and to the Ephesians* (Eerdmans, Grand Rapids, 1984), 88n223.

[9] Ben Witherington, *The Letters to Philemon, the Colossians and the Ephesians*, (Eerdmans, Grand Rapids, 2007), 148.

BROTHERS – AND SISTERS – WE ARE PROFESSIONALS!

John Piper, a distinguished American Baptist minister, wrote a bestselling book entitled *Brothers, We Are Not Professional*. The very first paragraph set the tone:

> We pastors are being killed by the professionalising of the pastoral ministry. The mentality of the professional is not the mentality of the prophet. It is not the mentality of the slave of Christ. Professionalism has nothing to do with the essence and heart of the Christian ministry. The more professional we long to be, the more spiritual death we will leave in our wake. For there is no professional childlikeness (Matt. 18:3); there is no professional tender-heartedness (Eph. 4:32); there is no professional panting after God (Ps. 42:1).[1]

He went on: 'The professionalisation of the ministry is a constant threat to the offense of the gospel. It is a threat to the profoundly spiritual nature of our work. I have seen it often: the love of professionalism (parity among the world's professionals) kills a man's belief that he is sent by God to save people from hell and to make them Christ-exalting spiritual aliens in the world. The world sets the agenda of the professional man; God sets the agenda of the spiritual man. The strong wine of Jesus Christ explodes the wineskins of professionalism … God, deliver us from professionalisers!'[2]

As one who throughout his ministry sought to be professional, I resent such language. I resent too the charge that those who seek

---

[1] John Piper, *Brothers we are not professionals* (B & H Publishing, Nashville, Tennessee, revised edition, 2013), 1.
[2] John Piper, *Brothers we are not professionals*, 3.

to serve the Lord in a professional manner fail to give their all to God. The reason why I sought to be a professional was because I wanted to give my very best to God. I wonder, would John Piper be happy to engage the services of an 'unprofessional' surgeon? The very thought is a nonsense!

Unfortunately, the term professional has been misunderstood. For some it implies unspirituality: a 'professional' minister serves God for the money rather than living out a calling. It is also thought to imply 'one-man' ministry: 'professional' ministers are deemed to be people who block the 'laity' from using the gifts God has given them.[3]

The roots of the first objection are found in the Old Testament, where the 'true' prophet receives a special calling from God in contrast to the institutional prophet and priest. For instance, Amos said to Amaziah: 'I am no prophet, nor a prophet's son; but I am a herdsman, and a dresser of sycamore trees, and the Lord took me from following the flock. And the Lord said to me, 'Go, prophesy to my people Israel' (Amos 7:14, 15). Similarly Jeremiah inveighed against the false prophets who had not 'stood in the council of the Lord so as to see and to hear his word' (Jer. 23:18); 'both prophet and priest are ungodly; even in my house I have found their wickedness', the Lord declares (Jer. 23:11: see also 5:13; 6:13, 14). However, the fact that ministers are remunerated does not mean they have been corrupted. There is nothing unspiritual about being paid for services rendered. As Jesus said, 'the labourer deserves to be paid' (Luke 10:10). Indeed, one could argue that a true professional is a labourer who is genuinely worthy of his hire.

As for the unhelpful association of 'one-man' ministry, it is true that the 'professional' ministry has often thought itself omnicompetent and in consequence left little to the 'laity' to do other than tolling the bell and taking up the collection. In this sense George Bernard Shaw was right when he drily commented, 'All professions are conspiracies against the laity'.[4] However, rightly understood professionalism has nothing to do with restrictive

---

[3] See also J. T. Miller, H. Robinson and P. L. Sampson, *So You Want To Be a Baptist Minister* (Baptist Union of Scotland, Glasgow, undated), 9: 'A very real danger in the Christian ministry is that of wearing the cloak of professionalism. It is possible for familiarity with sacred things to breed contempt for them in the heart … The warmth of a close walk with God will ward off the frosts of professionalism.'

[4] George Bernard Shaw, *The Doctor's Dilemma* (London, 1906).

practices, but simply seeks to encourage good working practices. Professionalism in ministry does not deny that God has gifted all his people for ministry, but seeks to encourage ministers to fulfil their role to the best of their ability (see Eph. 4:11-12)

More positively, we need to realise that the English word 'professional' stems from the medieval Latin word *professio*, which was used of the taking of vows upon entering a religious order. Gradually the word broadened in its usage and came to indicate 'a vocation in which a professed knowledge of some department of learning or science is used in its application to the affairs of others or in the practice of an art founded upon it'.[5] Here the emphasis is upon the term 'knowledge': not knowledge for its own sake, but knowledge applied in the service of others. In the context of Christian ministry, therefore, the word professional relates to the solemn ordination vows taken by ministers, who – in a Baptist context – promised 'with all fidelity, to preach and teach the word of God from the Holy Scriptures, to lead the congregation in worship and administer the gospel sacraments, to tend the flock of Christ and to do the work of an evangelist'. They also promised 'to be faithful in prayer and in the reading and study of the Holy Scriptures, and to lead a life worthy of the calling to which you have been called'.[6] So my desire to be a professional has been rooted in my desire to be faithful to the vows I took at my ordination.

Ministers seeking to be professional have first and foremost God in view. Writing to the church in Corinth, Paul said: 'Whatever you do, do everything for the glory of God' (1 Cor. 10:31). Later when writing to the church in Colossae, he said: 'Whatever you do … do everything in the name of the Lord Jesus' (Col. 3:17) - or as Eugene Peterson renders this verse: 'Let every detail in your lives … be done in the name of the Master, Jesus' (*The Message*).

Many an old church building has on it the initials ADMG, which stands for the Latin tag, *Ad Majorem Dei Gloriam* – 'For the greater glory of God'. This is what professionalism within a Christian context is all about. It is about giving our best for God; going the extra mile for God; always seeking to improve for God;

---

[5] *Oxford English Dictionary.*
[6] Ernest A. Payne and Stephen F. Winward, *Orders and Prayers for Church Worship: A Manual for Ministers* (Baptist Union of Great Britain, 4th edition, London, 1967), 219.

living out our call! ADMG should be the mark of every Christian's ministry. There is nothing cold and unspiritual about seeking to be professional — rather professionalism rightly understand is an expression of love of and passion for Jesus Christ. To decry professionalism runs the risk of endorsing mediocrity rather than excellence, sloppiness rather than carefulness, laziness rather than industry, the second-best rather than the best.

A BOOK A WEEK KEEPS A MINISTER AWAKE

Rick Warren, the founding pastor of Saddleback Community Church wrote:

> If you've ever been to Israel, you know there's a real contrast between the Sea of Galilee and the Dead Sea. The Sea of Galilee is full of water and full of life. There are trees and vegetation. They still do commercial fishing there. But the Dead Sea is just that – dead. There are no fish in it and no life around it. The Sea of Galilee is at the top of Israel and receives waters from the mountains of Lebanon. They all come into the top of it and then it gives out at the bottom. That water flows down through the Jordan River and enters the Dead Sea. The Dead Sea takes in, but it never gives out. That's why it's stagnant. The point is, there must be a balance in our lives to stay fresh with both input and output. There's got to be an inflow and an outflow. Somebody has said, 'When your output exceeds your income your upkeep will be your downfall'. There must be a balance. Most Christians get too much input and not enough output. They attend Bible study after Bible study. They're always taking in but they're never doing any ministry. The problem we pastors and church leaders face is the opposite. You're always giving out, and if you don't get input, you'll dry up.'[1]

Centuries ago Solomon began his collection of proverbs by highlighting the importance of wisdom: 'A wise man will hear and increase learning, and a man of understanding will attain wise counsel' (Prov. 1:5 AV) – or in the NRSV translation: 'Let the wise

---

[1] *To be a great leader, you absolutely must be a reader* (October 23, 2014)

hear and gain in learning and the discerning acquire skill'. It is true that in the first place these words are an encouragement to read the proverbs Solomon had collected : 'There's something here also for seasoned men and women, still a thing or two for the experienced to learn' (Eugene Peterson, *The Message*). However, this injunction can be applied to the reading of books in general. Indeed, A. W. Tozer, based a sermon on Proverbs 1:5 entitled, 'Read or get out of ministry'.

Tozer was quoting John Wesley, who used to tell his young ministers to 'read or get out of ministry'. What is more, Wesley modelled what he preached: he always used to ride with a book propped against his saddle pommel as he travelled from one engagement to another. Tozer also told of an American Indian preacher, who encouraged his hearers to improve their minds for the honour of God by saying: 'When you are chopping wood and you have a dull axe you must work all the harder to cut the log. A sharp axe makes easy work. So sharpen your axe all you can.'

Oswald Sanders also quoted John Wesley with approval:

> The man who desires to grow spiritually and intellectually will be constantly at his books. The lawyer who desires to succeed in his profession must keep abreast of important cases and changes in the law. The medical practitioner must follow the constantly changing discoveries in his field. Even so the spiritual leader must master God's Word and its principles, and know as well what is going on in the minds of those who look to him for guidance. To achieve these ends, he must, hand in hand with his personal contacts, engage in a course of selective reading.[2]

It was with this understanding of the importance of continuing learning that ministers used to call the room in which they worked their 'study'. Today, however, many ministers refer to their place of work as their 'office', which derives from a Latin word referring to the 'performance of a task'. I fear that this change of terminology points to a different understanding of ministry. As John Stott similarly reflected: 'Many are essentially administrators, whose

---

[2] A. W. Tozer, *Spiritual Leadership* (Marshall Morgan & Scott, London, 1967), 95.

symbols are the office rather than the study, and the telephone [now we should say "the computer"] rather than the Bible'.[3]

Ministers need to read. In the first place they need to read and study their Bibles. They also need to read and study more broadly. C. H. Spurgeon had a large personal library and believed passionately in the importance of reading. Commenting on Paul's words to Timothy, 'Bring the books, and above all the parchments' (2 Tim. 4:13), Spurgeon wrote: 'He is inspired, yet he wants books. He has been preaching at least thirty years, yet he wants books. He's seen the Lord, yet he wants books. He's had a wider experience than most men, yet he wants books. He's been caught up to heaven and has heard things that are unlawful to utter, yet he wants books. He's written a major part of the New Testament, yet he wants books.'

Ministers need to read more broadly. To quote Rick Warren again: 'Leaders are readers. Every leader is a reader. Not all readers are leaders, but all leaders are readers. A lot of people read but they're not leaders. If you're going to lead, you've got to be thinking further in advance than the people that you're leading.' Warren advanced four reasons for reading:

1. We must read for inspiration and motivation
2. We must read to sharpen our skills
3. We must read to learn from others
4. We must read to stay current in a changing world

I am suggesting ministers should aim to read a book a week. If that seems too ambitious, then what about this statement I came across: 'Every preacher in normal health ought to read from fifteen to fifty books a year and know them'! I believe that ministry would be revolutionised if every minister read at least one book a month. For many life seems too busy. Yet that is surely a question of priorities. If something is important, there is always time.

So how does this work out in terms of actual time? Oswald Sanders suggested that every minister should 'determine' (I like that word) to spend a minimum of half-an-hour a day in reading. John Stott expected more of ministers:

---

[3] John Stott, *I Believe in Preaching* (Hodder & Stoughton, London), 124.

Every day at least one hour; every week one morning, afternoon, or evening; every month a full day; every year a week. Set out like this it sounds very little ... Yet everybody who tries it is surprised to discover how much reading can be done within such a disciplined framework. It totals up to nearly 600 hours in the course of a year.'[4]

John Stott was writing as a single man, and some might therefore argue that he failed to understand the pressures experienced by ministers with families. But this is no reason to totally dismiss his pattern, while recognising that every minister needs to develop a pattern which works for them. I think of a minister friend who used to get up at 5 o'clock every morning to read for an hour or so before the day began. It has been said 'The person who has a comfortable chair in a quiet corner beside which is always a book with a marker and who reads twenty minutes after dinner and before retiring will read dozens of books each year.'[5] Alternatively, what about an annual reading week, either alone or with a group of peers?

The fact is that despite all the pressures upon them, ministers need to make time to read – they need to read for their own pleasure, for their own profit, and for the sake of the people they serve.

---

[4] John Stott, *I believe in Preaching*, 127
[5] Fred Craddock, *Preaching*, (Abingdon, Nashville; 1985; 2nd edition, 2000), 79.

ANNUAL REVIEWS ARE TO BE WELCOMED

In most work situations in Britain, annual appraisals have become a way of life, when employees have an opportunity, on an individual basis, to sit down with their line manager and review their past performance with a view to setting fresh goals for the following year. This formal exercise gives an opportunity for the line manager to give affirmation and to say 'well done'; to provide a safe environment for discussing problems; to identify training needs; and if necessary to rewrite the job description with new emphases; and to determine career prospects.

It is my conviction that appraisals, or what in a church setting I prefer to call 'reviews', should be a way of life for ministers. Certainly, for the twenty-one years of my ministry in Chelmsford it was a way of life for me. Indeed, before I arrived in Chelmsford, in determining the terms of ministerial settlement I took the initiative to ask for an annual review.

There are, however, major differences between ministerial reviews and workplace appraisals.

1. Many ministers do not have a written job description. Some years ago in a survey of 141 ministers in mainline Protestant churches I found that 77 per cent did not have a 'meaningful' job description.[1] It is assumed that everyone knows what ministers do and what is required of them, but the reality is that there are various approaches to ministry. In such a context ministers need to draw up their own job descriptions to form the basis for an annual review. It could

---

[1] Paul Beasley-Murray, *Power for God's Sake* (Paternoster, Carlisle, 1998), 58.

be quite enlightening for some lay leaders to understand what their ministers perceive their task to be.

2. Although paid by the church, technically ministers are 'office holders': this means that in the eyes of the law they are accountable to God alone. Yet I would argue that ministers have also a moral obligation to give an account of their ministry to those who have appointed them. In that regard, if the word 'love' in 1 John 4:20 is changed to 'accountable', we find, 'We cannot be accountable to God whom we have not seen, of we are not willing to be accountable to our brother and sister whom we have seen'!

3. In most churches there is no other person with experience in ministry to conduct the review. In such a situation having lay leaders take part in the review of their minister is tantamount to medical receptionists taking part in a review of the GP for whom they work. For that reason, in some of the more hierarchical denominations 'line' review conducted by an archdeacon or equivalent is the norm. The drawback then is that the review is inevitably based on second-hand knowledge. I have come to believe that review should be conducted by two representative lay leaders from within the church, along with an external ministerial facilitator (e.g. a hospital chaplain).

4. In a way which is less true of the workplace, 'the 'performance' of the minister tends to be bound up with the 'performance' of the church, with the result that it is difficult to review the one without the other. 'To separate the ministry of one Christian, namely the pastor, for evaluation,' wrote Jill Hudson, 'without considering the ministry of those with whom he or she shares the work of a particular congregation is not only unjust but theologically unsound'.[2] One possibility would be to conduct a review of the church's ministry at the same time as the review

---

[2] Jill M. Hudson, *Evaluating Ministry: Principles & Processes for Clergy & Congregations* (Alban, Bethesda, 1992), 7.

of the minister, but to do this on an annual basis would involve a good deal of work.

5. Whereas in the workplace annual appraisal can lead to promotion or to better pay or other benefits, this is not normally true of ministerial review. However, one key benefit common to both workplace appraisal and to ministerial review is that it allows opportunity for self-development.

Despite the differences between the secular workplace and ministry, I found that, without exception, my annual reviews were amazingly positive experiences – so much so that I came to look forward to the annual review. Indeed, annual review is probably more helpful to ministers than almost any other group of people. For ministry is by and large a lonely profession. Unlike other professionals, most ministers do not work in teams: they are on their own. True, they are part of a local church, but most lay leaders have no real idea of what is involved in the day-to-day ministry of their ministers. Even in my own case, where I always worked with other ministerial colleagues, there was the inevitable 'loneliness' of being the leader of the ministry team. What a difference it made to be able to share in confidence some of the pressures I faced. Annual review can break down isolationism and in so doing prove to be extremely supportive.

My experience has led me to conclude that reviews work best if the following actions are taken:

1. The lead is taken by an external ministerial facilitator who knows from first-hand experience what ministry is all about. I can remember one or two occasions when a problem had arisen and where the benefit of the facilitator's experience was important.

2. The internal representatives are limited to two lay leaders from within the church. Initially I tried to involve all my deacons and even sought to get feed-back from others in the church, but this complicated the process without adding any additional benefit

3. The interview (between the minister and those involved in the review) is limited to two hours maximum: 1.5 hours can be quite sufficient. I look back with embarrassment to an early experience of review which involved a series of meetings spaced over a whole Saturday.

4. The review is based upon the minister's own self-appraisal (together with proposals for future ministry and self-development) circulated prior to the interview. At an early stage I asked for those reviewing me to circulate prior to the meeting their own reflections on my 'performance', but this proved unduly bureaucratic.

5. The annual review is not an opportunity to spring major surprises on the minister. The relationship between the minister and his lay leaders should be such that, if there have been longstanding concerns relating to the ministry, then these should have already been raised in earlier feedback.

6. The review process is kept confidential. Nothing should be relayed back to other members of the leadership team unless the person being reviewed has given express agreement.

7. To ensure clarity, outcomes which may have been agreed at the interview should subsequently be put into writing and then formally agreed.

Annual reviews are in the interests of both the minister and the church. To express the matter theologically:

> Evaluation is natural to the human experience. Evaluation is one of God's ways of bringing the history of the past into dialogue with the hope for the future. Without confession of sin there is no reconciliation; without the counting of blessings there is no thanksgiving; without the acknowledgement of accomplishments there is no celebration; without awareness of potential there is no hope; without hope there is no desire for growth; without desire for growth the past will dwarf the future. We are called into new growth and new ministries by taking a realistic and hopeful look at what we have been and

what we can still become. Surrounded by God's grace and the crowd of witnesses in the faith, we can look at our past unafraid and from its insights eagerly face the future with new possibilities.[3]

Annual reviews are certainly to be welcomed!

---

[3] From a pamphlet prepared by the Division of Ordained Ministry of the United Methodist Church, quoted by Jill M. Hudson, *Evaluating Ministry: Principles and Processes for Clergy and Congregations* (Alban Institute, Washington D.C., 1992), 7.

CMD IS NOT AN OPTION

In their Foreword to *Guidelines for the Professional Conduct of the Clergy* the Archbishops of Canterbury and York wrote: 'The care of souls and the proclamation of the gospel are demanding roles, but profoundly fulfilling. If we are to be effective, we need to take proper care to refresh our learning and to refresh ourselves.'[1] I was struck not just by the emphasis on refreshing ourselves, but on refreshing our learning: the two go hand in hand. Continual ministerial development (CMD) is a means of sustaining ministry.

The fact is that there is no such person as a 'fully trained' minister. The three or so years at theological college are only a springboard for a life devoted to learning. Theological college marks only the primary stage of theological formation. There are many more stages yet to come, as ministers review and reflect on their ministry and discover fresh resources for ministry. In this process CMD is not an option. It does not matter how much study and experience ministers may have behind them, there is always more to learn. In a fast-changing world they need regular in-service training. Continual updating of personal and professional skills is a 'must' if ministers are not to be 'happy amateurs'.

The need for CMD seems obvious. Yet, despite all the encouragement, many ministers are reluctant to take advantage of attending courses and engaging in further learning. Roy Oswald quoted some American statistics to the effect that 'only 20 per cent of clergy in the US engage in regular continuing education events of five days or more each year'.[2] As far as British ministers are concerned, in 2017 I discovered from a survey of over 300

---

[1] *Guidelines for the Professional Conduct of the Clergy* (Church House, London 2nd edition, 2015) vii.
[2] Roy Oswald, *Clergy Self-Care* (Alban, Washington D.C. 1991), 12.

Baptist ministers that 31 per cent had bought two or less books in the last six months, and that 9 per cent had not bought a book at all. In addition, over half do not set aside any specific time in the week for reading related to ministry. Furthermore, although the terms of ministerial settlement recommended by the Baptist Union of Great Britain state that ministers are entitled to a week of study or reading, most did not avail themselves of such a week. To be precise, in response to the question 'Over the last three years or so how many reading weeks (or equivalent) have you taken?', the responses were: 56% none; 15% one week; 10 per cent two weeks; and 20 per cent three weeks.[3]

How does one motivate more ministers to engage in CMD? There are no Scriptures which explicitly commend life-long learning. However, the words of Jesus found are instructive: 'You are not to be called rabbi, for you have one teacher, and you are all students' (Matt. 23:8 NRSV). The actual word here is not 'students' but 'brothers' (*adelphoi*), a translation adopted by the NIV & REB. However, in the context the NRSV translation gets to the heart of what Jesus said: even the 'doctors of the church' are but students – or 'classmates' as Eugene Peterson in *The Message* renders the term.

We could also point to the importance that the Apostle Paul had for reading. Writing to Timothy, Paul said, 'When you come ... bring the books, and above all the parchments' (2 Tim. 3:14). The 'books' were probably papyrus rolls containing parts of the Old Testament; the 'parchments' may have been his personal 'notebooks' (REB) in which Paul wrote down and reflected upon his experience of ministry.[4]

However, it would probably be more effective to follow the example of Baptists in New Zealand and Scotland where engagement in CMD is linked with ongoing accreditation. But whether the many independent-minded Baptist ministers in the larger Baptist Union of Great Britain would accept such a compulsory scheme, I am not sure. I doubt too whether the Baptist Union of Great Britain has the financial resources for implementing and monitoring such a scheme.

---

[3] See Paul Beasley-Murray, 'Ministers' Reading Habits', *Baptist Quarterly* 49 (January 2018).
[4] See Paul Beasley-Murray, 'A model pastoral theologian', *Church Matters*, 2 October 2014.

In the meantime, I commend the CMD programme developed by the College of Baptist Ministers which encourages its members to create a personal portfolio based on the nine strands (listed alphabetically rather than in order of importance):

1. Accountability: regularly opening our lives to the supportive scrutiny of one or two others.

2. Applied Practice: gaining new insights through reflecting on our experience of ministry and church life, learning through failure as well as success, pioneering new ways of doing mission and ministry, creating courses that help our people grow in their faith, becoming more effective as a preacher, developing new skills in managing change, resolving conflict, building team, and in leading God's people forward

3. Collegiality: meeting together with other ministers to strengthen, encourage and support one another.

4. Learning: through attending courses, reading books, working for a formal qualification, or simply going on a broadening sabbatical.

5. Ministry Opportunities: this is a strand introduced with retired ministers in mind, where they can list the various 'ministry' activities' (e.g. preaching, leading a mid-week home group, mentoring, and pastoral care)

6. Practical Competencies: relating to some of the more practical competencies of ministry identified by the Baptist Union of Great Britain, such as IT skills and safeguarding policies

7. Review: on an annual basis allowing others to help us review our ministries, affirming all that has been positive in the past year, and agreeing the shape of ministry for the coming year.

8. Spirituality: sustaining and deepening our walk with God.

9. 'Other': a catch all category where a wide range of activities may be listed which perhaps have very little to do with the church, but nonetheless enrich the minister as a person

Members are encouraged to post regularly brief date-marked entries according to the strands: over the year members are expected to put something in every strand. Apart from the spirituality strand, which is difficult to assess, each experience of development has to be linked to a way in which it could be confirmed, for the rare occasion where verification could be helpful to the minister. As a member of the College of Baptist Ministers I first began to develop a portfolio in April 2012 and have found it a useful framework and have appreciated the sense of accountability which it brings.

In conclusion, CMD is just another way of speaking of the need to commit to a life-long process of learning and growing. In this sense, CMD is not an option!

MINISTERS ARE MADE BY THEIR FELLOW LEADERS

Some years ago, I wrote a little book entitled *Radical Leaders: A guide for elders and deacons in Baptist churches*.[1] It contains the following dedication: 'In appreciation of all those deacons who have served with me in my churches in Altrincham and Chelmsford. To a large degree I am what I am because of them.' I am very grateful for the difference my deacons made to me.

Yet Baptist deacons have often had a bad press. Gerald Coates, the leader of the Pioneer 'house churches', caricatured deacons when he wrote: 'Resist the devil and he will flee from you – resist the deacons and they will fly at you.'[2] Similarly, it has been said that 'Deacons can make Herod look compassionate.' But in almost 35 years of pastoral ministry, my experience has been very different. Over the years I have served with scores of deacons, but of these men and women only two made life difficult for me, and both eventually apologised for their behaviour.

Another critic of Baptist churches was Michael Saward, a former canon of St Paul's Cathedral, who wrote: 'Free or Independent churches tend to reduce the position of the minister ... to that of one who fulfils their wishes. It takes a very fine church (or an especially able minister) to avoid that trap, which may be why relatively few major exciting reforms seem to have come out of the British nonconformist tradition in recent years.'[3] Although there were individual members who wanted me to act as their

---

[1] Paul Beasley-Murray, *Radical Leaders: A guide for elders and deacons in Baptist churches* (Baptist Union of Great Britain, 2005; 2nd edition, 2005).

[2] Gerald Coates, *What on Earth is this Kingdom* (Kingsway, Eastbourne, 1983).

[3] Michael Saward, *All Change* (Hodder & Stoughton, London, 1983), 30.

personal chaplain, I thank God that this was never the attitude of deacons with whom I served. They always encouraged me in the lead I sought to give, and only questioned my lead if they thought I might be about to commit an extremely grave error! I never left a meeting angry or frustrated by their obstructiveness.

Clearly deacons do a disservice to their minister if they are simply a group of 'yes' men and women. The leadership of a church is the better where differences of viewpoint can be expressed, provided that these differences are not allowed to become personal. Time and again I found the truth of the proverb: 'Iron sharpens iron, and one person sharpens the wits of another' (Prov. 7:17). As Bruce Waltke commented: 'The analogy infers that the friend persists and does not shy away from constructive criticism. This persistent friend, whose wounds are faithful (v. 6), is the opposite of the fawning neighbour (v. 14) and the cantankerous wife (vv. 15-16) and performs an indispensable task. As a result of his having a 'hard' friend – a true one – a man develops the capacity to succeed in his tasks as an effective tool, and in the end he will thank his friend for being hard as flint.'[4] Within the context of a leadership team, even the most gifted of leaders need other leaders around them. My ministry was enriched as a result of working with other leaders, whether they were deacons or ministry team members. I shared my dreams and visions with my leaders and was blessed by their creative response, which often caused me to re-think and re-shape my ideas.

In this regard let me quote Joseph Hellerman, a New Testament scholar who at the same time was involved in church leadership and wrote a book on *Embracing Shared Ministry*:

> No individual has a corner on the truth. We all know this in theory. Yet the way we implement the senior pastor model too often results in one person's vision and teaching style determining the practical realities of day-to-day ministry in the local church. The model works marginally well, if the pastor happens to be an emotionally healthy person who opens up his life to a handful of other persons in the congregation. Unfortunately, this kind of relational maturity

---

[4] Bruce Waltke, *The Book of Proverbs: Chapters 15-31* (Eerdmans, Grand Rapids, 2005), 384.

is less and less common among young seminarians preparing for the ministry'.[5]

'The corporate approach to congregational life has led all too often to an insecure, narcissistic leader acquiring unilateral authority over the rest of the community, enabled by a church board whose metrics for ministerial success does nothing to curb the unhealthy behaviour of their gifted but relationally challenged leader. The systemic weaknesses of what we might call 'corporate ecclesiology' have converged to open the door to the abuse of power and authority by numbers of persons in vocational Christian service.[6]

I was grateful for those fellow leaders who felt free to challenge me'. It was precisely through the clash of ideas that progress was often made. It is in the powerful exchange of ideas that 'people learn from one another' (Prov. 27:17 GNB). A church is the stronger precisely if its leadership team is made up of disparate people who are not all in the minister's mould.

I know that my experience is not everybody's experience. I remember one minister saying that if he were to win the lottery, he would tell his deacons to 'go to hell', and then leave the church! I am mindful of another minister friend who was forced out of his church by two deacons who felt his performance was lacking. I recognise too that there are churches where the minister has been regarded as the paid servant of the church, there to fulfil the whim of the congregation. But this was not my experience. In both my churches I had the joy of working together with deacons who, while willing to question, were supportive of my leadership. I thank God for their wisdom and encouragement, which played a key role in my leadership development.

---

[5] Joseph Hellerman, *Embracing Shared Ministry: Power and Status in the Early Church and why it matters today* (Kregel, Grand Rapids, Michigan, 2013), 235.
[6] Hellerman, *Embracing Shared Ministry*, 292.

DISCIPLINE IS THE OTHER SIDE OF DISCIPLESHIP

'Discipline is the other side of discipleship' said Henri Nouwen, a Dutch Roman Catholic priest, who in addition to sharing his life with people with disabilities, wrote widely on the spiritual life. Nouwen went on to say:

> Discipleship without discipline is like waiting to run in the marathon without ever practicing. Discipline without discipleship is like always practicing for the marathon but never participating. It is important, however, to realise that discipline in the spiritual life is not the same as discipline in sports. Discipline in sports is the concentrated effort to master the body so that it can obey the mind better. Discipline in the spiritual life is the concentrated effort to create the space and time where God can become our master and where we can respond freely to God's guidance. Thus, discipline is the creation of boundaries that keep time and space open for God. Solitude requires discipline, worship requires discipline, caring for others requires discipline. They all ask us to set apart a time and a place where God's gracious presence can be acknowledged and responded to.' spiritual life without discipline is impossible.'[1]

As ever, Jesus is our ultimate model. Jesus knew what it was like to be under pressure. A day such as that described in Mark 1:16-32 would have exhausted even the fittest. Yet Jesus did not succumb to these pressures. Jesus retained his spiritual vitality and authority

---

[1] Henri Nouwen, 'An Invitation to the Spiritual Life', *Leadership* XII (Summer 1981), 57. See also Henri Nouwen, *Making Things New: An invitation to the spiritual life* (HarperCollins, 1998)

as a result of a disciplined life of prayer. 'In the morning, while it was still very dark, he got up and went out to a deserted place and there he prayed' (Mark 1:35). The Gospels indicate this was no exceptional occasion, but that retreating for prayer was a regular part of his devotional pattern (see Luke 6:12). Only in this way could Jesus get his priorities right. With Matt. 4:31-42 in mind, Bruce Epperly drew upon a modern analogy:

> Perhaps Jesus was tempted by the adulation inspired by his success as a teacher and healer to stay in Capernaum. He needed to still every voice but God's voice speaking within his own experience to discern the next steps of his journey. Jesus needed to realign his spiritual GPS. What was true of Jesus must be true of us: we too must pause to discern the direction we need to go.[2]

Jesus lived a balanced life – a life of action and prayer. Likewise, the followers of Jesus, and not least ministers, need to live balanced lives. We need to live balanced lives to survive, for otherwise we will be crushed by the pressures of life, our spirits exhausted, our prayer life negligible, and our spiritual effectiveness nil. We need too to live balanced lives in order to be all that God would have us to be.

The precise shape of a disciplined life will vary from minister to minister. Christopher Ellis suggested that ministers adopt seven 'good practices and gracious disciplines': viz. worship, waiting on God, Sabbath keeping, reading Scripture, prayer, spiritual direction, and giving attention to the grace of God.[3] However, there is no one 'rule' of life. There is no one pattern of spirituality. What is vital is that each minister has a rule.[4] As Frederick Bruner reminded us, 'only the life that gets aside, that closes the door occasionally, is usually able to live the rest of the day prayerfully'.[5]

---

[2] Bruce Epperly, 'Finding Your Spiritual GPS', *Alban Paper*, 13 April 2015.

[3] Christopher Ellis, 'Being a minister: spirituality and the pastor' in Pieter Lalleman (ed.), *Challenging to change: dialogues with a radical Baptist theologian* (Spurgeon's College, London, 2009).

[4] See Harold Miller, *Finding a Personal Rule of Life* (Grove, Nottingham 1984) 4-5: 'By embracing Rule, we make for ourselves a standard which we would like to attach, by the power of the Spirit, and we are enabled from time to time to do some appropriate assessment of where we have got to … Rule is merely a means to an end, and the end for me is that we might walk closely with God, and live more effectively for him.'

[5] Frederick Dale Bruner, *The Christbook: Matthew 1-12* (Eerdmans, Grand Rapids, Michigan, 2004), 288.

To 'sustain the weary with a word', we need 'morning by morning... to listen as those who are taught' (Isaiah 54:4).[6] Although some are more 'owls' than 'larks', nonetheless every minister needs to make time at the beginning of the day to be consciously in the presence of God. To live the life Christ has called us to, we need to begin the day with prayer. 'The prayer of the morning', wrote Dietrich Bonhoeffer, 'will determine the day. Wasted time, which we are ashamed of, temptations that beset us, weakness and listlessness in our work, disorder and indiscipline in our thinking and our relations with other people, very frequently have their cause in the neglect of the morning prayer.'[7] Michael Henshall, a former Bishop of Warrington who always got up early in the morning to pray, called this 'the ministry of the morning' He went on: 'I recognise that what matters is not what time one rises, but what time one gives to God, whatever time one rises. I simply note that those who leave it late often leave it altogether.'[8]

My own custom for many years has been to begin the day by using the daily 'Anglican' lectionary: sometimes I read the set 'offices' of the day, with its two readings from the Old and New Testaments, but normally I stay with the three shorter passages set for 'Holy Communion' which always include part of a Psalm. The lectionary gives me a balanced diet, yet does not over-face me in terms of the amount. As I read, whenever a phrase or a verse jumps out at me, I mark my Bible; and then, for a shorter or longer period, I seek to chew over what God may be saying to me. Not infrequently this involves me pulling out a commentary or getting out my Greek New Testament: I find that in-depth study often proves to be a way into the presence of God himself.

From Scripture I turn to prayer. Here too I find the need for a system: I devised a simple plan for the week, with various categories for each day: when I was the minister of a church this would include my colleagues, my deacons, church activities, as well individuals for whom I had promised to pray; there was a section

---

[6] Barry Webb, *The Message of Isaiah* (IVP, Leicester 1996) 198: 'The Servant... is a skilled counsellor because he himself has been taught by the Lord. He is a disciple before he is anything else, and as such his outstanding characteristic is attentiveness to God.'

[7] Dietrich Bonhoeffer, *Life Together* (SCM, London, 1954), 53.

[8] Michael and Nicholas Henshall, *Dear Nicholas* (Sacristy Press, Durham 2nd edition, 2019), 27.

too for life beyond the local church, as well as 'catch all' sections such as 'Yesterday', 'Today', and 'Special Needs' In 'retirement' some of the categories are different: I remember former younger colleagues as well as members of the retired ministers' fellowship which I lead; I have listed too the names of those who belong to my home group and those who are part of my Rotary club. For me part of the daily discipline involves having a system.

My experience is that without discipline my discipleship is not what God would have it be. In that respect I discovered that some ministers appear to lack any system. For my survey of the reading habits of Baptist ministers revealed that of the 309 respondents 13 per cent used the Lectionary, 38 per cent used printed or online Bible notes; 55 per cent read through a Bible book either with or without a commentary; while as many as 19 cent had no regular pattern of Bible reading. Without wanting to appear to be legalistic, all I can say is that without the discipline of 'rule' of life, my walk with God would suffer.

LONG PASTORATES HAVE REAL ADVANTAGES

It has been said of pastoral ministry: 'The first two years you can do nothing wrong. The third and fourth years you can do nothing right. The fifth and sixth years of a ministry, either you leave or the people who think you can do nothing right, leave. Or you change, or they change, or you both change. Productive ministry emerges somewhere in the seventh year or beyond.'[1] Similarly, in a survey of 350 Baptist churches Alan Wilkinson and I tested the fruitfulness of long-term ministry in one church and found that 'it is not until a minister has served for five to ten years in his church that a bias towards growth becomes evident. In other words, it takes time for fruit to emerge from someone's leadership'.[2] This finding was subsequently confirmed by Peter Brierley who, on the basis of an analysis of 3000 churches, found that:

1. Leaders staying less than six years are the most likely to see their congregations decline.

2. Leaders staying for between 7 and 13 years are those most likely to see their congregation grow.

3. Leaders staying longer than 15-17 years are likely to see their congregations decline.

4. There are many brilliant exceptions in churches where leaders have served for more than 20, 30 or even 40 years or more with great success.[3]

---

[1] Lynn Anderson: 'Why I've Stayed', *Leadership* VII. 3, 77.
[2] Paul Beasley-Murray and Alan Wilkinson, *Turning the Tide*, 34.
3 Peter Brierley, 'The Optimum Length of Ministry', *Future First*, February 2013.

Yet many ministers do not stay long enough to enjoy the fruits of their ministry. In Britain, for instance, Methodist ministers tend to stay only five years in any given circuit; while the average length of a Baptist minister's pastorate is around six years.[4] In the USA the average pastoral tenure is substantially shorter and tends to be around four years.[5]

By contrast I had the joy of two long pastorates: at Altrincham I served for over thirteen years; while in in Chelmsford I served for twenty-one years. Both churches experienced substantial growth. In Altrincham, in spite of high mobility, the membership quadrupled in size. In Chelmsford, the church which had at one stage declined to a membership of 260, ended up with a committed membership of 400.

There are times when staying for the long-term is not advantageous either to the minister or the church. There is no point for a minister to remain in a church where the members refuse to follow the leadership offered; nor is there any point in remaining in a church where it quickly becomes apparent that one is a square peg in a round hole. Nor is anything to be gained if a minister fails to grow and develop with the result that sermons become dry and the church's life becomes stagnant.

Yet, in spite of such *caveats*, there is much to be said for pastoral longevity. American research into the Long-Term Pastorate (LTP), defined as more than ten years, showed that:

- An LTP makes possible greater in-depth knowledge of and relationships between the pastor and individual church members as well as between clergy and the congregation as a whole;
- Experiencing an LTP makes possible cumulative developing knowledge and experience of each other for both clergy and congregation, as they observe and participate in each other's growth over time;

---

[4] Figures for Baptist ministers were gained from studying the *2013 Directory* (Baptist Union of Great Britain).

[5] See George Barna, *Today's Pastors* (Regal Books, Ventura, California 1993) 36-37. A 2011 research poll from Lifeway Research suggested the average American pastor's tenure in a local church is 3.6 years: see further Franklin Drummond, 'How long do pastors stay in one church', posted 26 June 2014 on the General Baptist website: www.gbjournal.

- Greater continuity and stability of leadership and program in an LTP makes possible events not possible during a short tenure;
- An LTP opens up possibilities of greater personal and spiritual growth for both clergy and congregation;
- An LTP makes possible greater in-depth knowledge of and relationships between the pastor and individual church members as well as between clergy and the congregation as a whole;
- An LTP makes possible deeper knowledge of and participation by the clergy in the community (local, professional, ecumenical, larger denominational); and
- An LTP allows additional personal benefits for both the clergy and his/her family.[6]

The researchers concluded:

> In many ways, maintaining a healthy long pastorate is more difficult than changing pastorates every five to eight years. Clergy can dazzle and even fool a congregation over shorter periods of ministry. Many simply repeat their five-year bag of tricks everywhere they go. In a long pastorate people get to know their clergy very well, both their assets and their liabilities. These clergy either need to be genuine, authentic persons who live by what they preach and advocate or, to the detriment of their ministry, they are soon found out. It is definitely easier to be the spiritual mentor of people over the short haul than over the long haul. In a long pastorate, clergy soon exhaust whatever wisdom or knowledge they brought to the scene and must continue to scramble to grow personally or end up repeating themselves and boring others. But those who do grow, who do monitor the other disadvantages of a long pastorate, will be likely to have a ministry that is very rewarding and fulfilling.[7]

---

[6] Roy M. Oswald, Gail D. Hinand, William Chris Hobgood and Barton M. Lloyd, *New Visions For The Long Pastorate*, Alban Washington DC, 1983), 29, 30.

[7] *New Visions for the Long Pastorate*, 87.

I have found long-term ministry extremely rewarding and fulfilling. It's a wonderful privilege to be involved in families over a period of time and to see those children brought for a service of dedication later confess their own faith in baptism; and then at a later stage to be involved in their marriage and even in the dedication of their children. There can be great gains in family stability: my own children benefited no end from spending their formative years in one happy church. There are also great gains in the development of deep and meaningful friendships: constantly shifting from one place to another can lead to ministers and their spouses experiencing fairly shallow relationships.

In the words of Eugene Peterson, what is needed to counter 'church hopping' is 'a long obedience in the same direction'.[8]

---

[8] See Eugene Peterson, *A Long Obedience in the Same Direction: Discipleship in an Instant Society* (IVP, Downers Grove, 2nd edition 2000) 201, 202. The phrase 'a long obedience in the same direction' actually comes from Friedrich Nietzsche who wrote: 'The essential things 'in heaven and earth' is .. that there should be long obedience in the same direction; there thereby results, and has always resulted in the long run, something which has made life worth living' (*Beyond Good and Evil*, English Translation London 1907, section 188).

FEW CHURCHES ARE IMMUNE FROM POWER GAMES

Christians suffer from a considerable degree of naivety, if not self-inflicted blindness. We know that power games are a reality in the world of politics and in the world of business, but we do not want to accept that they are also a reality in the church. Yet why should the church in this respect be any different from the world? If all the other sins of the 'flesh' are to be found in the church, then why not this one? Any intelligent reading of the New Testament would reveal that there were power struggles right from the beginning of the life of the early church. One recalls not only James and John, anxious to sit on the right and left hand of Jesus in his glory, but also the Judaisers who wanted to impose their way of doing church on the Gentile converts, the bickering factions at Corinth. It is scarcely an exaggeration to say that within every strand of the New Testament we can find evidence of power struggles affecting the life of God's people. Yet time and again we seem to close our eyes to this underlying reality and prefer to live with an 'ideal' picture of the church.

For instance, when I was training for ministry, I was never warned of power games and conflict. As one educationalist commented: 'The church so talked about in seminary is neat, tidy and generally civilised'; yet in reality 'A particular congregation is never neat, sometimes barely Christian, and only rarely civilised'.[1]

Of course, there are overt power struggles in churches, which hit the national headlines, and which are therefore recognised by all and sundry. In the North American scene one such public power

---

[1] Denham Grierson, *Transforming A People of God* (Joint Board of Christian Education of Australia & New Zealand, 1985) 18; quoted by Martyn Percy (ed.), *The Study of Ministry* (SPCK, London 2019).

struggle took place in the early 1990s at First Baptist Church Dallas, then perhaps the most influential church in America. Joel Gregory after his losing the battle with W.A. Criswell, told of how he came to see that:

> The church ... is an institution divine in its original foundation but tethered to this celestial ball by every frailty to which humans are subject. Covetousness, littleness, jealousy, lust for power, ego, sacrilege, and a hundred other demons all lurk within the hallways ...
>
> The church on earth at its best is a crippled institution that God may elect to use for His purposes. The divinisation of the church in an egotistic triumphalism denigrates the very purpose for which it is founded. After all, its founder died on the cross between two felons. Out of his weakness came strength and out of His death came life. Humanity does not consider Jesus Christ its centrepiece because he behaved like the CEO of a gigantic ecclesiastical corporation. He washed the feet of others; He did not trample them under His own in the name of God.[2]

Although First Baptist Church, Dallas, was exceptional in the way in which the clerical wrangling was made so damagingly public, the infighting itself is not so exceptional. Struggles for power and influence are the bread-and-butter diet of many a church, even though such struggles may carry pious labels. In a survey of 151 ministers in mainline Protestant churches, one in five reported that their churches were racked by power politics of one kind or another.[3] As I look back on my ministry, although my first church was unusually free of power games, my time as principal of Spurgeon's College was over-shadowed by power struggles, while in my second church the first few years were marred by what Lyle Schaller, a distinguished American church consultant, called 'the AAEOL Club': i.e. Angry Alienated Ex Old Leaders who opposed every change. According to Schaller:

---

[2] Joel Gregory, *Too Great A Temptation* (The Summit Group, Fort Worth, Texas, 1994), 324.
[3] Paul Beasley-Murray, *Power for God's Sake: Power and Abuse in the Local Church* (Paternoster, Carlisle, 1998), 107.

> While their numbers rarely exceed one or two or three %,
> the members of this informal 'club' (it usually meets without
> prior announcement in a member's home) often can be highly
> vocal in articulating their unhappiness with the growing sea of
> strange faces they see around them in church![4]

As a result of my experience I fully concur with Richard Holloway,
a former Bishop of Edinburgh, who wrote:

> Churches can be cockpits of conflict; deeply neurotic places
> where people play power games and deny the reality of
> their own circumstances. I have witnessed these things and
> been part of the strange collusion that allows churches to be
> extremely dishonest places.[5]

Power struggles take place at various levels. In some churches
ministers are pawns in the hands of their church boards or become
the victims of a small but powerful faction within the church. In
other churches it is not the minister who is abused, but the members
of the church who are abused in the sense that power is perverted,
people are manipulated, families are divided, and casualties abound.
An unhealthy dependence of members on the leadership develops
and ultimately creates total spiritual confusion in their lives. The
leaders of such churches so mesmerise their followers that, for a
while at least, their leadership is accepted without question.

Time and again power is misused and people are abused in
Christian churches and institutions. The travesty is that power
is exercised as though it were for God's sake, even although the
real underlying issues may have nothing to do with God himself.
To make matters worse, because Christian faith is a matter of life
and death, there is often a peculiar intensity surrounding power
and power struggles in the church. The bitterness of Christian infighting is to be experienced to be believed. Would that God could
at times be left outside the situation!

Many have been deeply wounded. The wounds have been so
deep and the pain so intense that large numbers have left the

---

[4] Lyle Schaller, *The Pastor and the People* (Abingdon, Nashville, 2nd edition, 1986) 165.
[5] Richard Holloway in *Churches and How to Survive Them* (HarperCollins, London, 1994) by Richard
Holloway and Brice Avery, xiv.

church altogether. Indeed, it is not simply those who have been abused who have left, but also those who have seen friends and loved ones abused. This experience of the abuse of power in the church has been so devastating that many have given up on God altogether. Others may still retain their faith in God, but although they may not have given up on God, they most certainly have given up on his people. And who would blame them? In the words of one placard: 'Those who make it hardest to be a Christian in this world are often the other Christians.'

Furthermore, such power games seriously hinder the church in its mission and growth. To quote Lyle Schaller again:

> On any given day in perhaps three-quarters of all churches the ministry of that congregation is reduced significantly as a result of non-productive conflict. In perhaps one fourth of all churches that internal conflict is so sufficiently severe that it must be reduced before the parish can redirect its energies and resources towards formulating new goals and expanding its ministry.[6]

The mission of the church is not just affected by mis-directed and mis-spent energy. The very fact that power games are being played is a negative witness to those outside the church. Warring and abusive factions in the church undermine the credibility of the Christian faith.

Ultimately the only way in which the problem of power games can be addressed, is for churches and their leaders to focus on Jesus and the example he set. 'Let the same mind be in you that was in Christ Jesus', wrote Paul to the Philippians, and thereupon cited that great Christ-hymn, which tells of how the Lord Jesus emptied himself of all his rights and privileges in order to serve the purposes of God (Phil. 2:5-11). Jesus reversed all human ideas of greatness and rank, and in so doing unleashed in an unparalleled way the power of God into our world. Power for God's sake is power surrendered in the service of others.

---

[6] Lyle E. Schaller in his Foreword to *Leadership and Conflict* (Abingdon, Nashville, 1982) by Speed Leas.

A SOUL FRIEND ENCOURAGES INTEGRITY

Of all the seven deadly sins, 'sloth' is the most archaic of names. The dictionary defines sloth as 'laziness, indolence'. However, when the monks talked of sloth (the technical term is '*accidie*') they did not have in mind the refusal of one of their number to pull his weight in doing whatever might have been his task. Sloth was a term for spiritual apathy; a spiritual listlessness which had more to do with prayer rather than with work. A slothful monk might go through the motions of being religious, attending all the services of the day, but in fact he had given up on the heart of religion, he had given up on cultivating his relationship with God; indeed, he might as well have given up on God himself. In other words, sloth is a refusal to continue to grow in God; it is a form of spiritual laziness.

Justine Allain-Chapman called sloth 'the vice of the pastor':

> It is a lack of self-care, lack of attention to growth and struggle and the discipline involved in doing so. Afflicted by this vice, the pastor falls asleep, and so is lazy or throws him- or herself into busyness, often expressed in taking on other people's problems. Both extremes fail to reach those who need a good pastor to discern what is needful for their situation.[1]

Sloth is much more than mere indolence. According to William Stafford, to call sloth 'indolence' is 'like calling viral pneumonia a cold'.[2] It can perhaps be likened to the 'mid-ministry blues'.

---

[1] Justine Allain-Chapman, *Resilient Pastors: The Role of Adversity in Healing and Growth* (SPCK, London, 2012), 131.
[2] William Stafford, *Disordered Lives:* Healing the Seven Deadly Sins (Cowley Publications, Boston, 1994), 110.

Mid-life is a time when idealism meets realism. The former is well characterised by Ray Ragsdale: 'Most ministers begin their careers with lofty ideals and high expectations. Their commitment is to serve God and humankind, and there is just enough of the *messiah complex* in the young to believe they are going to change the world before they are done'.[3] But with the passing of the years such idealism normally fails to deliver the goods. Mega-status is not for most of us. The mid-ministry blues is often also linked with seeing one's peers, some of whom apparently less gifted than ourselves, receiving the call to larger churches. To quote one cynical minister: 'Thirst for career status, measured in terms of membership, staff size, and church location, makes for a subtle rat race in which ministers vie with one another under a smoke screen of piosity'.[4] It can prove spiritually and emotionally debilitating when one fails to make it in this ministerial rat race.

My observation is there are a good number of ministers who have succumbed to the mid-ministry blues. Although they may not have physically left the ministry, in their hearts they have opted out. Burnt-out and disillusioned, their earlier joy and enthusiasm for pastoral ministry had long since gone. Satisfaction, if gained at all, is found outside the normal routines of ministerial life such as in some special involvement in the community, or in sitting on some denominational board, or engaging in some theological research project. Clearly there is nothing wrong with any such interest. Indeed, there is a lot to be said for ministers pursuing an interest beyond the local church. But if such interests dominate and become the all-consuming passion, then there is cause for concern: the health of the ministry is in jeopardy where men and women are no longer in love with their calling, however busy they may be.

Or maybe 'mid ministry blues' is not the best of descriptions. Perhaps we should use terms such as dejection, despair, spiritual depression – which in turn cause ministers to fail to live up to their calling. They have lost their sense of self-worth – or in the words of William Stafford, 'some clergy know that they are failures in the deepest sense, paralysed by their own spiritual mediocrity'.[5]

---

[3] Ray W. Ragsdale, *The Midlife Crisis of a Minister* (Word Books, Waco, 1978), 40.
[4] Quoted by Ragsdale *The Midlife Crisis of a Minister*, 41.
[5] William Stafford, *Disordered Lives*, 112.

But, enough of other ministers. The reality is that there have been times when all ministers, myself included, have succumbed to one form or another of the deadly sin of sloth. What then should we do? The answer is found in an address given to clergy wives by Jean Coggan, the wife of the former Archbishop Donald Coggan, entitled *Who helps the Helpers?* The title was taken from one of Juvenal's satires, where Juvenal literally said, 'Who is to watch over those who are doing the watching?'[6] In its original context this had something to do with a woman who comes to entice the guard. Jean Coggan applied this to those involved in pastoral work:

> The time comes when we [the helpers] have lifted too many burdens and we really are worn down, exhausted, and depressed. Maybe our faith is cold and also our lives and witness for the Lord. Perhaps we feel we are in a dark tunnel. Depression comes over us. What then?[7]

In this description of a spiritual sickness which we might call 'sloth' or *accidie*, the answer is clear: friends are needed who will provide help through the dark and difficult patches of ministry; friends who will strengthen our hand in God (see 1 Sam. 22:15). For some such friends can be found in 'peer' groups, who support one another through holding one another accountable. For myself, I tended to look to individual 'soul friends' to hold me accountable. In my first church it was a college principal, who regularly asked me awkward questions about my prayer life. When I became a college principal, I used to 'bare my soul' to an Anglican nun. In my second church I met with a Cambridge don who had developed a ministry of spiritual direction.

These meetings with 'soul friends' of one kind or another were not always easy experiences. For as Thomas Merton wrote:

> The whole purpose of spiritual direction is to penetrate beneath the surface of a [person's] life, to get behind the façade of conventional gestures and attitudes which s/he presents to the world, and to bring out his/her inner spiritual freedom,

---

[6] Juvenal, *Satires*, 6, 1:347.
[7] Jean Coggan, *Who helps the Helpers?* (Care & Counsel, London, undated).

his/her inmost truth, which is what we call the likeness of Christ in his/her soul.'[8]

Spiritual direction, rightly exercised, brings to the surface our feelings and thoughts and in the process can expose false motives. At times this can be painful, precisely because the real 'person' emerges. However, it is only as the inner self is exposed to God's light and love that there is any hope for growth and development in the Christian life. For me the fact that I was accountable to a spiritual director for my walk with the Lord gave my ministry integrity. It meant an end to ministerial 'play-acting'. It ensured that the inevitable discontinuity between the public expression and the private realities of my spirituality were kept to the minimum.

I thank God for those 'soul friends' who helped me deal with sloth and kept me on the pilgrim way.

---

[8] Thomas Merton, *Spiritual Direction and Meditation* (The Liturgical Press, St Joseph, Minnesota, 1960) 16, quoted by Peter Madsen Gubi, *Spiritual Accompaniment and Counselling: Journeying with psyche and soul* (Jessica Kingsley, London, 2015), 29.

MONDAY MORNING BLUES
ARE PAR FOR THE COURSE

As I write, it's Monday and I feel fine. What's more, I went to church yesterday morning, and I still feel fine. I even gave a 15-minute presentation at Breakfast with the Bible, and that too has made no difference to my mood. I feel great and look forward to the rest of the week!

How different things are to when I was a minister of a church. Then I would often feel incredibly depressed. Some Mondays I could have almost wept. And yet there was no rational reason for my sadness and depression; indeed, normally there was every reason why I should have been grateful to God for the way in which Sunday had gone. Nonetheless Mondays often were bad days.

On a regular basis I suffered from what I used to call the Monday morning 'blues'. Or is that the right term? To my surprise I discovered that the Monday 'blues' describe a set of negative emotions that many people get at the beginning of the working week if they're not happy at work. According to Rita Friedman, a Philadelphia-based career coach: 'If you love your job and are passionate about what you're doing, going in to work Monday morning is another opportunity to do what you love. But if you're feeling under-appreciated or unsatisfied with your job, it can be especially difficult to start another seemingly endless workweek.'

If that is the case, I didn't suffer from the Monday blues. I loved my 'job' and felt amazingly privileged to be paid by God's people to serve as the minister of a church. As for Sunday, it was the best day of the week. What could be better than leading God's people in worship, expounding God's word, and then meeting up with friends old and new immediately after the service?

Yet, on Monday mornings I often felt desperate. Why? What was the cause of my Monday morning blues? I believe it was a physical, emotional and even a spiritual reaction to the 'high' of the Sunday. All the past week I had been building up to Sunday. On Sunday itself I would experience what the medics call a major adrenaline 'rush', but on Monday I would often experience an adrenaline 'crash'.

Let me explain a little more. Every week there were sermons to prepare – and then to deliver. In one sense it was reminiscent of my Cambridge days, when as a student every week I had to write a couple of essays. But the discipline of writing a sermon is very different from writing an essay: for it involves more than the mind, it involves the heart and the soul. What is more, preaching a sermon is a totally different experience from reading an essay to a tutor: for in preaching we are appealing not just to the minds, but to the hearts and souls of our hearers. Preaching is not just giving a 'thought for the day': it is a passionate proclamation of the good news of God's love for us all in Jesus. Preaching is not about God and twenty minutes: rather through our preaching we are trusting that God will change the lives of our listeners. As a preacher I was very conscious that I was dealing with eternal issues – the sense of responsibility could at times be overwhelming.

Then along with the sermons to prepare, there were services to 'craft'. Services do not just happen. This is particularly true in Nonconformist churches where there is no prayer book to fall back upon. From start to finish creativity is called upon. An experienced Australian Baptist minister with a thousand-strong congregation used to speak of the weekly 'show' he put on for his people. Some people found his description of worship offensive, and perhaps understandably so. First and foremost, worship is about acknowledging God's worth and has nothing to do with impressing others. Yet precisely because ministers are seeking to enable others to enter God's presence, this can involve a massive amount of preparation. Hymns and songs have to be chosen, Bible readings selected, prayers crafted, interviews put together. True, others may be involved, but nonetheless ultimate responsibility for the shaping of the service falls upon the minister.

Preaching God's Word and leading God's people in worship can be enormously demanding – let alone all the pastoral conversations that often take place on a Sunday. It involves a total giving of oneself This is the reason for ministers experiencing the Monday morning blues. They are par for the course, as is indicated by a host of articles which can be found on the web, one of which is ironically entitled, 'Monday morning blues – the pastor's weekly wreck'![1]

So what can ministers do to help themselves on a Monday morning? Traditionally Monday has been the minister's day off. As a result some ministers spend the day on the golf course and no doubt work out any frustrations resulting from the previous day by hitting the ball extra hard! However, in a situation where formally I was allowed just one day off a week, I was loathe to use as my free day the day when I felt worst. Instead I took off Friday as my free day. I dealt with my Monday 'blues' by consciously adopting a number of 'self-care' strategies: on Monday mornings I would cheer myself up by meeting with my staff; on Monday afternoons I would often spend time allowing God to speak into my life by doing the basic commentary work for the following Sunday's sermons; and on Monday evenings as an extravert I would often draw energy from interacting with 'the punters' at an Alpha supper.

Ultimately what helped me was to realise that Monday 'blues' are just par for the course. A degree of self-awareness can be a great help in coping with the weekly low of a Monday morning.

---

[1] www.academic.edu, originally published in *Voice: An Independent Church Journal* (July 2011) by M. Scott Bashoor.

THANK GOD FOR FRIENDS!

Strange as it may seem to some, friendship can be an issue in ministry. I have heard experienced ministers question the rightness of ministers having friends within their own church. Close friendships, some say, can ignite jealousy in a church; they can become a threat to confidentiality; and they allow a small coterie of individuals to have an undue influence on the ministry. Some maintain that this is a price of ministry: if ministers are to be friends of all, then they cannot afford to be special friends of some. Ministers, it is said, are by definition 'lonely set-apart people'[1] and cannot afford to have deep meaningful relationships within their church.

I acknowledge that there is a point to this argument. For a minister to be seen to make a distinction between one group of people and another cannot be right. As the followers of Jesus, we are called to be friends of all: not just those who are very much part of the church, but also those who are on the margins of the church. Indeed, if anything we are called to prioritise those who have yet to belong to the church. Paul Fromberg, rector of an Episcopalian church in San Francisco, expressed the dilemma which he faced every Sunday: 'I want to talk to the people I already know, those who are already my friends, but I see first-time visitors hanging around the edges … But the commitment that I have made to looking for friendship in those I do not already know moves me out of the comfortable place of spending time with known friends. And so, I turn to the one I do not know and seek the image of God

---

[1] Margaretta Bowers, cited by Rowland Croucher, *Renewal in the Pastorate* (D. Min dissertation, Fuller Theological Seminary, Pasadena, California, 1983).

that they bear.'[2] Ministers by the very nature of their calling are be available to all.

Nonetheless, I believe there is a place for ministers having close friends within the church. Ministers are human and their very humanity means that they need friends. No man is an island', declared John Donne.[3] We are made to relate to others. 'It is not good for the man to be alone' (Gen. 2:18 NRSV) declared the Lord God. We are made for friendship. To restrict close friendships to relationships outside the church is unnatural and unfair. Over the years Caroline and I have had discreet close friendships within our churches and have been immensely grateful for the support these friends have offered to us and to our family.

For some people friendship in the church is about knowing people's names and having a friendly chat before or after the Sunday morning service. However, true friendship is about sharing our life together. This kind of friendship is not to be confused with Facebook friendship which involves sharing photos and experiences. True friendship is much deeper. It is about being open and real with one another.

I am grateful for the many true friends that we have had over the years. As I said in my speech at our Golden Wedding: 'If it be true that "Love is blind; but friendship closes its eyes", then many of you have closed your eyes. Yes, we have been blessed with friends, who have known all about us, but still have liked us. In the words of Prov. 18:24 "Some friends play at friendship, but a true friend sticks closer than one's nearest kin".'

We have been grateful in particular for friendship when the going has been tough. How right Spurgeon was when he said: 'Friendship is one of the sweetest joys of life. Many might have failed beneath the bitterness of their trial had they not found a friend.'[4] Or in the words of Henri Nouwen:

> When we honestly ask ourselves which person in our lives means the most to us, we often find that it is those who, instead of giving advice, solutions, or cures, have chosen rather to

---

[2] Paul Fromberg, *The Art of Transformation* (Church House Publishing, New York, 2017), 62.
[3] John Donne, *Meditation* XVII (1624).
[4] Charles Haddon Spurgeon, 'The Friend of God', sermon preached in the Metropolitan Tabernacle, London, 8 May 1887.

share our pain and touch our wounds with a warm and tender hand. The friend who can be silent with us in a moment of despair or confusion, who can stay with us in an hour of grief and bereavement, who can tolerate not knowing, not curing, not healing and face with us the reality of our powerlessness, that is a friend who cares.'[5]

Although the Bible doesn't say very much about friendship, it does provide one great example of friendship, viz. the friendship between Jonathan and David. I find it significant that as part of their friendship they made a 'covenant' together (1 Sam. 18:3,4); or in the words of the GNB: 'Jonathan swore eternal friendship with David because of his deep affection for him'. As a result of that covenant, when David was under pressure due to opposition from Saul, Jonathan went out to him and 'strengthened his hand in God' (1 Sam 23:15, 16). By contrast the naming of Winnie the Pooh as the United Nations Ambassador of Friendship in 1998 was incredibly trivial, even though Winnie the Pooh once said: 'If you live to be a 100, I want to live to be a hundred minus one day, so I never have to live without you.' I thank God for real friends – not 'Winnie the Pooh friends', but 'Jonathan friends'.

Friends make all the difference to living. I cannot imagine life without them. To quote Jesus, Son of Sirach: 'Faithful friends are a sturdy shelter; whoever finds one has found a treasure. Faithful friends are beyond price; no amount can balance their worth. Faithful friends are life-saving medicine; and those who fear the Lord find them' (Sir. 6:14-16).

[5] Henri Nouwen, *Out of Solitude: Three Meditations on the Christian Life* (1973)

THANK GOD FOR FAMILY!

More than fifty years ago, on Saturday 26 August 1967, Caroline and I pledged our love and commitment to one another, and what adventures we have had together since! Yes, I thank God for my family: for Caroline; for our children Jonathan, Timothy, Susannah and Benjamin, together with their 'spouses' Fiona, Charlotte, Rob and Kathryn; and, of course for the grandchildren – Sophie, Theo and David; Felix and Clara; Jemima and Raphi; and Agatha. Family is part of God's plan for creation, and despite the inevitable stresses and strains of family life, as Genesis 1 repeatedly declares, what God created is 'very good'

I like too the wording of the second creation account: 'Then the Lord said, "It is not good that the man should be alone. I will make him a helper as his Partner"' (Gen. 2:18). It reminds me of the magazine for wives of Baptist ministers and missionaries, which was called *The Helpmeet*, the word used by the AV to describe Eve's role. Although today's feminists would not approve of either term, the fact is that the Hebrew word underlying 'helper' or 'helpmeet' is a strong word, and in the Old Testament is used fifteen times to describe God. Indeed, according to Trevor Dennis, it 'almost always refers to one stronger than the one who needs the help'.[1] On reflection, what does that say about the relationship of ministers and their wives?

As an important aside (and therefore not just relegated to a footnote), I need to make clear that although I am here primarily

---

[1] See Trevor Dennis, *Sarah Laughed: Women's Voices in the Old Testament* (SPCK, London, 1994) 12. According to Phyllis Trible, *God and the Rhetoric of Sexuality* (Fortress Press, Philadelphia), the word for 'helper' would be better translated 'companion'. 'Helper', she said, too easily suggests to us a position of inferiority and subservience, whereas the Hebrew word behind the second part of the phrase implies that the creature God is looking for will be on a par with the man, his counterpart not his lackey, his colleague rather than an under-gardener who just deals with the rubbish and spreads the manure.

writing about ministers' wives, this is not because I believe there is no place for women in ministry. As I have written at length elsewhere, 'Leadership is a gift for women too! ... The hierarches of Jew over against Gentile, of slave over against free, of male against female, no longer exist in Christ (Gal. 3:28). In Christ a revolution has taken place. The old order has passed away, a new order has come.'[2] However, although Baptists have had women ministers for over eighty years, currently only some 13 per cent of their ministers are women. With 30 per cent of students preparing for Baptist ministry now women, the imbalance between men and women will gradually improve. But when I began my ministry, and throughout most of my ministry, Baptist ministers' husbands were relatively few. This is the context within which this chapter is written.

To return to my more general theme, from the very beginning of our relationship, Caroline knew I was heading for ministry and therefore knew her destiny was to be a minister's wife. I thank God for the way that she accepted that calling – for calling it is, and not just a role. Over the years that role changed. In our first church in Altrincham she was highly involved in church life: along with being president of the women's meeting and chair of the Ladies Coffee Evening, she ran three Bible studies a week for women, and was normally present at both the morning and evening Sunday services. Later, however, she went to the Bar and then became a coroner, and her role in the church changed. Apart from chairing the management committee of a child contact centre, her Christian service was almost exclusively in the world beyond the church. But she still retained her calling as a minister's wife, and for that I am grateful. What a difference it makes if a minister's wife can be a true 'partner' (GNB) or 'companion' (NRSV), sharing a common 'yoke' (Phil. 4:3).

There are times, however, when this 'yoke' is not easy. Being a minister's wife can be a tough calling. This was illustrated in the responses I received from 141 ministers to the question 'Has pastoring this church been difficult on your family?' 23 per cent said 'definitely' (rising to 33 per cent of those in larger churches);

---

[2] Paul Beasley-Murray, *Living Out the Call II: Leading God's People*, 10-12.

49 per cent said 'to some extent'; and only 26 per cent said 'no'.[3]

As I commented at the time: 'It would have been interesting if ministers' wives had answered this question, the likelihood is that the figures would have been higher. The fact is that the pressures faced by most ministerial families are considerably higher than other domestic set-ups. The phenomenon of having to live in a kind of goldfish bowl, where the life of the pastor and of the pastor's family is continually on display, can be highly stressful.'

I noted too the comments of an Anglican bishop, who listed other ways in which clergy families are different from other families: tied housing, few resources, moral standards, public image to keep up; expectation of ideal family, ill-defined boundaries between work and home life, and doing the Lord's work with spouses having to compete with God.[4]

In addition, there is having to handle the heartache of criticism of one's husband. in the words of one minister's wife: 'If you are criticised in a secular place of work, it hurts but you leave those people behind when you go home at the end of the working day. Not so in church life, especially when your friends are the wives of the very deacons/leaders who are not seeing eye to eye with your husband for whatever reason.'[5]

That life can be difficult for ministers' wives came out too in my 2018 survey of retired Baptist ministers. In answer to the question, 'Would your spouse want to be married to a Baptist minister?' a quarter of respondents were 'unsure' while others thought 'probably not'. 'My spouse would share my own ambivalence in respect of the experience of having been in Baptist ministry', said one; 'my wife found, at times, the expectations hard', said another; 'it was a stressful experience', said a third. Almost 6 per cent said their wives definitely would not wish to be married to a Baptist minister: 'The expectations were overwhelming'; 'Forty years of ministerial life has taken its toll and while my wife still has a strong firm faith in God she does not want to be involved in a Baptist

---

[3] Paul Beasley-Murray, *Power for God's Sake*, 39.

[4] See Mary Kirk and Tom Leary, *Holy Matrimony? An exploration of marriage & ministry* (Lynx, Oxford, 1994), 39, 40.

[5] See 'Fallen from Grace: when things go wrong for a clergy wife (*Ministry Today* 13, 1998) 12-15 written anonymously by a minister's wife who found she had to leave her husband.

church, or any church for that matter'. One spouse commented: 'the church takes over your whole life, the pay and conditions were not good, and the children lost out when the church came first. I saw my husband suffer too much.'[6]

Life can also be difficult for ministers' children. In response to the question 'Would your children want to be involved again in church life?' only a third (34 per cent) gave an unequivocal 'Yes', others were less positive. A number said that while some of their children had good experience of church, other children in their family had 'a complete turn-off'. One replied: 'one of our children turned away from church, but not from Jesus Christ, because of the mismatch between faith and Christian behaviour towards me in some leading Christians at a key time in his life'. Over a quarter (26 per cent) were unsure: 'Who knows? Sadly, they are not involved with church now, but they do have good memories of some of the things they did as part of a church'. Almost 10 per cent said their children would definitely not want to be involved in church life – 'they were badly burnt' said one; another regretted the extent to which his children were affected by times of extreme tension'; another mentioned the unhelpful expectations that some church members have of ministers' children. Disturbingly just under half (49 per cent) of the children of the ministers in this survey were still involved in church life.[7]

Ministry can be tough for the 'children of the Manse'.[8] As I wrote in my autobiography: 'There are great advantages to being a PK [Pastor's Kid] to develop self-confidence and social skills. It's not surprising that many PKs do well in life and contribute much to society. But life is not always easy for PKs. There are times when churches abuse their pastors, and in so doing they abuse the children too. I fear for leaders of such churches when they have to stand at the last judgment and give an account of the way in which they treated the 'little ones' in their care (see Matt. 18:6). Sadly, many PKs have been driven out of the church.'[9]

In terms of our own family, our children had a wonderful experience of church life in my first church. Indeed, 'There was

---

[6] See Paul Beasley-Murray, *Retirement Matters for Ministers,* (College of Baptist Ministers, Chelmsford, 54-55:

[7] Paul Beasley-Murray, *Retirement Matters for Ministers*, 55, 56.

[8] Paul Beasley-Murray, *This is my story*, 99.

[9] Paul Beasley-Murray, *This is my story*, 11.

no better place for the family to grow up'. However, later they had a very bad experience of Christian life: as one of my children at the time said, 'If this is institutional religion, then you can stuff it'. Thankfully, although God's people let us down, our children have not. Thank God for families!

MINISTRY HAS ITS STAGES

Some models of ministerial development are depressing. Charles Stewart divided the period of active ministry into three stages:[1]

1. Career Establishment (26-45)

2. Maintenance (45-60)

3. Decline (60-retirement).

A little less depressing was the model offered by the Southern Baptist *Minister's Personal Management Manual* where the adult period of an individual's developmental process was divided into four stages:[2]

1. Start-Up Stage (From about 15-25)

2. Stabilisation Stage (From about 25-40)

3. Summit Stage (From about 40-55)

4. Sunset Stage (From about 55-)

Thankfully, there are more positive models for the stages of ministry. Andrew Blackwood in his aptly entitled book, *The Growing Minister* divided the period of active ministry into three stages:

1. Years full of promise (25-40)

2. A period of transition (40-55)

3. A time of fruition (55-70)[3]

It is true that Blackwood was cautious about the second stage. For although 'a man normally expects to keep maturing throughout

---

1 Charles Stewart, *Person and Profession: Career Development in the Ministry* (Abingdon, Nashville ,1974).

[2] Truman Brown (ed.), *Minister's Personal Management Manual* (Convention Press, Nashville, 1988), 58.

[3] Andrew W. Blackwood, *The Growing Minister: His Opportunities and Obstacles* (Abingdon, Nashville, 1960), 152-166.

middle age', he noted that 'in the ministry the reverse is often true… More ministers seem to make shipwreck, or get stranded, during middle age than at any other period. Much as we talk and think about the perils of a young clergyman, we ought to feel more concern about 'the destruction that wasteth at noonday'.'[4] Blackwood referred to the 'double DD.' of 'Disillusion and Discouragement, Despondency and Despair'. However, according to Blackwood, even for the minister who goes through the mid-ministry crisis, there is hope: 'By the grace of God a minister past fifty can right himself and then keep going on to the most fruitful and blessed portion of his entire career'.[5] Not surprisingly this led him on to say that 'the closing years of a full-time ministry ought to be the most fruitful of all, and the most joyous'.[6] He headed this section with the well-known lines from Browning's 'Rabbi Ben Ezra':

> *Grow old along with me!*
> *The best is yet to be,*
> *The last of life, for which the first was made!*
> *Our times are in His hand*
> *Who saith, 'A whole I planned,*
> *Youth shows but half; trust God, see all, nor be afraid!'*

Is this just wishful thinking? From first-hand experience I would argue that the final stage of ministry can be the best of years. Like vintage wine, with the passing of the years there is a richness and depth to ministry which was not there in the beginning.

True, with the ageing process, energy levels are not the same. When I was a young minister in my late 20s if a meeting at church finished by 9.30 pm, then I would go out visiting. I reckoned that I could always knock on the door of most people up until 10 pm – with my leaders I believed that I would be welcomed up until 10.30 pm! But once I became 60, if a meeting ended at 9.30 pm I was delighted to be able to go back home and read the paper! Initially I had difficulty in accepting the fact is that my energy levels were no longer what they once were. However, with the passage of time I

---

[4] Blackwood, *Growing Minister*, 156.
[5] Blackwood, *Growing Minister*, 157 expanding upon Psalm 91:6.
[6] Blackwood, *Growing Minister*, 159.

found myself taking the occasional power nap. If I had had a heavy day, and there was still work to do in the evening, I would often put my feet up and listen to the news, and almost immediately I would be lost to the world for 20 minutes. I used to feel guilty about such naps, until I listened to an Anglican cleric in his late 50s tell of how every day after lunch he went to bed for a siesta!

Another positive approach to ministry development was offered by Bruce and Katherine Epperly, who divided the stages of ministry into four seasons:

1. Springtime: 'The sense of call to ministry and seminary… when discernment of call and nurture of ministerial identity are central'.
2. Summer: 'The first congregational call, marked by adventure and tests of integrity'.
3. Autumn: 'Midcareer in ministry, with challenges of endurance and new opportunities for transformation'.
4. Winter: 'Retirement and the adventure beyond that require vision and letting go'.[7]

From my position as one who is no longer in stipendiary ministry, I like the way retirement is regarded as a season of ministry; I also warm to the description of retirement as an 'adventure'. However, to describe this as the season of winter feels to me somewhat bleak analogy. With Paul Tournier I prefer to liken retirement to the autumn of life.[8] Indeed, drawing upon the opening lines of John Keats' poem *To Autumn*, I suggest that it is the season of 'mellow fruitfulness'. Using the analogy of seasons and I would adapt the Epperlys' model as follows:

1. Springtime: The first congregational call, marked by adventure and tests of integrity.
2. Summer Midcareer in ministry, with challenges of endurance and new opportunities for transformation.

---

[7] Bruce G. Epperly and Katherine Gould Epperly, *Four Seasons of Ministry: Gathering a Harvest of Righteousness* (Alban, Herndon, Virginia, 2008).
[8] Paul Tournier, *The Seasons of Life* (English Translation, SCM, London, 1964).

3. Autumn: Retirement and the adventure of exploring ministry without leadership responsibilities

4. Winter: The final season of living out God's call, marked by weakness, but also by inner renewal and integrity.

Or to express these four stages of ministry without the seasonal analogy, the seasons are as follows:

1. The years of youthful energy and enthusiasm (25-45 years).

2. The years of growing maturity (45-65+years).

3. The years of wisdom and fruitfulness (65+ years –).

4. The years of contentment and letting go of everything but Christ.

It will be noted the final stage of ministry has no specific age reference. The entry into the final stage of life depends less upon age and more upon health.

RETIREMENT MARKS A MAJOR NEW STAGE IN MINISTRY

At first I struggled to call myself 'retired' – the English word 'retirement' has such negative connotations. According to the *Shorter Oxford English Dictionary*, to 'retire' means to 'withdraw', to 'retreat', to 'give ground', to 'cease to compete'. In one sense that is true: retirement does involve a leaving of office or of employment. Yet, as I have discovered, it is also about new beginnings and new opportunities. A poem which sums up my experience of retirement is *The Terminus*, written by David Adam, the former Vicar of the Holy Island of Lindisfarne.[1]

> *The Terminus is not where we stay,*
> *It is the beginning of a new journey.*
> *It is where we reach out beyond,*
> *where we experience new adventures.*
> *It is where we get off to enter new territory,*
> *to explore new horizons, to extend our whole being.*
> *It is a place touching the future.*
> *It opens up new vistas.*
> *It is the gateway to eternity.*

Although very much a new stage in life, for me, as indeed for most ministers, this is not the end of ministry. Rather retirement simply marks a new stage in ministry. Louis Armstrong, the great jazz musician, once said: 'Musicians don't retire; they stop when there's no more music in them'. That too is how most retired ministers feel: we still have divine music in our souls and we will only stop

---

[1] Written by David Adam for a greeting card published by Tim Tiley Ltd, Bristol.

giving voice to that music when we join the greater chorus in heaven![2] The God who called us into ministry still has a call on our lives.

True, we are no longer have a church to run and should let go of any desire to do so. Retirement is about letting go and entrusting the church to the Lord of the church. In this regard I found the following comment from an Anglican perspective most helpful: 'Priests never retire, but vicars do… They relinquish jobs, but not their vocations.'[3] Although Baptists do not refer to their ministers as 'priests', I find the use of this term here unusually meaningful. A priest by definition is a 'bridge' between God and the world. The Latin word for priest (*pontifex*) literally means 'bridge-builder'. I believe that part of my on-going calling has a 'priestly' aspect to it: in all that I am and do, I am called to serve as a 'bridge' between God and others.

Precisely how retired ministers live out their calling will vary from person to person; and it will vary too according to our health and strength. What retired ministers have in common is that we are free to serve God in new ways and 'on our own terms', without the expectations and pressures of church people.

Many retired ministers are still busily involved in serving God in his church. In a survey of retired Baptist ministers, I found that 85% continued to preach and lead Bible studies; 55% continued to take funerals from time to time; 47% helped with pastoral care; 36% led a home or small group; and 21% mentored younger ministers.[4]

Along with many other retired ministers of my age, I am still keen to use my experience and energy in the service of God. For instance, I continue to preach and teach; and I lead and host a home group. However, unlike most other retired ministers, for me one important way of living out my call and serving God has been devoting time to writing. In this period I have written *Living Out the Call;*[5] *This is my story; a story of life faith and ministry;*[6]

---

[2] I am grateful for this analogy to Canon Hugh Dibbens, who in retirement serves as the Evangelism Adviser in the Barking Episcopal Area of the Diocese of Chelmsford.

[3] Michael Butler and Ann Orbach, *Being Your Age: Pastoral Care for Older People* (SPCK, London, 1993), 48.

[4] *Retirement Matters for Ministers,* 83.

[5] *Living out the Call: 1. Living to God's Glory; 2. Leading God's Church; 3. Reaching God's World; 4. Serving God's People* (Feed-a-Read 2015; revised in 2016).

[6] *This is My Story: A story of life, faith and ministry* (Wipf & Stock, Eugene, Oregon, 2018).

Retirement Matters for Ministers;[7] *Entering New Territory*;[8] and *Make the Most of Retirement: a guide for ministers.*[9] Another key aspect of my current ministry is *Church Matters*, a weekly blog which I started in autumn 2011.[10] Every week I receive responses from all over the world: it is almost like having a virtual congregation, except that the blogs take the place of sermons. In addition, I wrote an 8000-word scholarly article on the reading habits of ministers, based on a survey of over 300 ministers.[11] In this period of retirement I have also revised a workbook for couples preparing for marriage[12] and a guide for the bereaved,[13] and edited eight volumes containing 512 articles previously published in *Ministry Today.*[14] This ministry of writing and research is just one particular way in which I seek to live out my call. Other retired ministers live out their call in other ways, whether it be through engagement in their local church or in service in the wider world beyond the church. There is no one pattern for ministry in retirement. What we have in common is that in one way or another we seek to be faithful to the call that God has on our lives.

I recognise that one day, unless God takes me early, I will make the transition from the 'third age' of active retirement to the 'fourth age' of dependency. However, at that stage I will still remain a minister. In this regard I identify with Paul Clayton: 'We are called not only to do God's work in the world, but also to be God's people in the world…. That identity is marked by integrity rather than greed, care for others rather than self-absorption, humility rather than arrogance.'[15] When illness strikes and death perhaps loom and there is nothing perhaps we can do, what counts is our 'witness

---

[7] *Retirement Matters for Ministers: a Report on a research project into how Baptist ministers experience retirement* (College of Baptist Ministers, 2018).

[8] *Entering New Territory: Why are retired Baptist ministers moving to Anglican churches? What are the underlying theological issues?* (College of Baptist Ministers, Chelmsford, 2019).

[9] *Make the Most of Retirement: a guide for ministers* (Bible Reading Fellowship, Abingdon, 2020).

[10] See www.paulbeasleymurray.com

[11] Paul Beasley-Murray, 'Ministers' Reading Habits', *Baptist Quarterly* 49 [1] (January 2018).

[12] *Happy Ever After? A Workbook for Couples Preparing for Marriage* (College of Baptist Ministers, Chelmsford 3rd edition, 2017).

[13] *A Loved One Dies: Help in the First Few Weeks* (College of Baptist Ministers, Chelmsford 2nd edition, 2018).

[14] *Ministry Today UK: 1994-2018* (College of Baptist Ministers, Chelmsford, 2018).

[15] Paul C. Clayton, *Called for Life: Finding Meaning in Retirement* (Alban, Herndon, Virginia, 2008) 88.

of courage and faith'.[16] I find myself greatly challenged by what Clayton had to say. Even at the end God will still have a call on my life. Retirement for ministers Is simply a new stage in ministry.

[16] Paul Clayton, *Called for Life*, 97.

NEVER GIVE UP

Perseverance, if not actually part of my DNA, was etched upon my soul from my earliest years. The motto of my primary school was 'Persevere'. My secondary school had a Latin motto which essentially said the same thing: *Vincit qui patitur* – 'the one who perseveres, conquers'. I even won a school prize for academic 'perseverance'. So very early in my life I was taught the importance of persevering, of sticking at a task, of maintaining a purpose despite difficulty or discouragement. In the words of Samuel Johnson, 'Great works are performed not by strength, but by perseverance'.[1]

What is true of life in general is also true of ministry: perseverance is a key virtue in ministry. It is the man or woman who 'sticks at it' who achieves the task. In *Dynamic Leadership*, written while I was principal of a college training men and women for ministry, I developed a list of 'six key qualities for pastoral leadership': viz. vision, enthusiasm, industry, humility, love – and perseverance. There I stated: 'It is the will to persevere that is often the difference between failure and success. The vision may be right, but the vision may not be easily realised'.[2]

I related the story of Thomas Sutcliffe Mort, who was determined to solve the problem of refrigeration so that meat could be exported from Australia to Britain. He gave himself three years in which to do it, but in fact it took him twenty-six years. He lived long enough to see the first shipment of refrigerated meat leave Sydney, but died before learning whether it had reached its destination safely. He had however lived long enough to realise his family motto: 'To

---

[1] Samuel Johnson, *The History of Rasselas, Prince of Abyssinia* (1759) chapter 13.
[2] Paul Beasley-Murray, *Dynamic Leadership*, 188,189.

persevere is to succeed' (a play on their Huguenot family name: *Fidele à la Mort!*).

I went on: 'Perseverance is necessary in Christian leadership not because of technical difficulties (which principally dogged Thomas Mort), but because of people difficulties. However right the vision, history has frequently proved that the people of God have sometimes been slow to catch the vision, and that process can take time. Perseverance allied to patience is needed.'[3]

There came a day, however, when I was tempted to give up. I was back in pastoral ministry and was leading the church into a redevelopment project. Most of my people agreed that we urgently needed to do something about our buildings, which were working against us rather than for us. Unfortunately, there was small vocal group in the church who bitterly opposed the project. This bitterness became very personal and I became the focus of a huge amount of criticism. Not surprisingly younger people – and older people too – left the church, despairing of a church that apparently could not live at peace with itself. It was an extraordinarily difficult time. Matters went from bad to worse when one of my deacons came to see me and told me he felt that God would have me leave the church; while another deacon threatened to move a vote of no confidence in me at the next church meeting. It was in this context of feeling a failure that I went on a week's personally guided retreat in the wilds of Norfolk. There every evening I was given three Scriptures to pray over and report back the following evening on what I believed God was saying to me. It proved to be an extraordinarily painful experience, for the retreat director was effectively using Scripture to scourge my soul. But ultimately it was a wonderfully releasing experience, for as I came to realise, I was being encouraged to 'look to Jesus' (Heb. 12:2,3), and to him alone. In this regard I found Eugene Peterson's paraphrase helpful:

> Keep your eyes on *Jesus*, who both began and finished this race we're in. Study how he did it. Because he never lost sight of where he was headed – that exhilarating finish in and with God – he could put up with anything along the way: cross, shame, whatever. And now he's *there*, in the place of

---

[3] Paul Beasley-Murray, *Dynamic Leadership*, 189.

honour, right alongside God. Whenever you find yourselves flagging in your faith, go over that story again, item by item, that long litany of hostility he plowed through. That will shoot adrenaline into your soul.' (*The Message*)

I returned home strengthened, with fresh spiritual reserves, determined not to give up but to persevere. With the passing of time that determination to persevere was vindicated: for not only was the building project completed, but the church was spiritually renewed as a direct result of laying its life on the line financially in order to complete the project. My first seven 'lean' years of ministry were followed by a further fourteen very happy years of ministry.

Perseverance, as I have personally discovered, is vital in ministry. We need to 'run with perseverance the race that is set before us' (Heb. 12:2 NRSV). The GNB translates the underlying Greek word (*hupomones*) as 'determination', but there is more to it than that, for 'endurance' is also involved. This concept of endurance is found in Paul's words to the leaders of the church at Ephesus: 'If only I may finish my course and the ministry that I received from the Lord Jesus, to testify to the good news of God's grace' (Acts 20:24). Paul likened ministry to a marathon race where what counts is not the initial sprint, but the stamina to keep going and finish the race;[4] he also likened ministry to a task (*diakonia*) given by the Lord Jesus which must be completed. The emphasis is on the finishing, 'not dropping out from exhaustion or getting disqualified along the way'.[5]

There are times when ministers of the Gospel need determination to stick at it and not give up. I love the example of William Carey, the great missionary pioneer, who toward the end of his life said to his nephew Eustace. 'I can plod. This is my only genius. I can persevere in any definite pursuit. To this I owe everything.'[6] So, let's resolve to never give up!

---

[4] The same idea is found in 1 Cor. 9:24-27; Gal. 2:2; Phil. 2:16; and 2 Tim. 4:7. Richard B. Hays, *First Corinthians* (John Knox Press, Louisville 1997) 156, commenting on 1 Cor. 9:24-27, had the delightful paraphrase: 'If these athletes push themselves to the limit in training to win that pathetic crown of withered vegetables, how much more should we maintain self-disciple for the sake of an imperishable crown?'

[5] David Bennett, *Metaphors of Christian Ministry* (Paternoster, Carlisle, 1993), 144.

[6] S. Pearce Carey, *William Carey* (Hodder & Stoughton, London, 1923), 28.

MINISTRY IS TOUGH BUT REWARDING

Ministry is tough and the ministerial honeymoon can be very short. The pressures on a minister can be intense – so intense that within the first three years of leaving theological college the majority of my year group had fallen out of ministry

In a survey I conducted in 1997 of 141 ministers drawn from all the mainline Protestant denominations, almost half of them (44 per cent) said they had been tempted to leave ministry. The pressures seemed to centre around three issues:

> The chief cause appeared to be power struggles of one kind or another. Ministers spoke of 'church politics and power', 'wrangles', 'struggles', 'difficulties' , 'problems', 'conflict with the leadership', 'a major split', 'the pain inflicted by Christians', 'open hostility especially as a woman', 'total resistance to change, however small, however gentle'.
>
> Associated with such power struggles, another reason frequently given was 'frustration', and the inability to get anywhere. Comments included 'not making much worthwhile headway in congregation', 'feeling ineffective', 'despair', 'sense of failure', 'lethargy of members of the church at times', and 'tears'.
>
> A third factor constantly mentioned was the 'pressure' of pastoral ministry. Such expressions as 'the holy rat race', 'pressure on family life', 'high expectations', and 'pressure to perform' were found. Likewise, mention was several times made of 'long hours' having to be worked.[1]

---

[1] *Power for God's Sake*, 37.

Many jobs in life are pressurised. However, in ministry, the pressures can be very personal. People can be very unkind. In the same survey ministers commented on the distress they had experienced as a result of seeking to lead God's church:[2]

stress	92%
hurt	83%
hurt experienced by spouse	76%
sleeping difficulties	57%
abuse of spouse/family	55%
poor health	44%
suicidal thoughts	10%
depression	9%
nightmares	7%

In this survey nine out of ten ministers said, 'churches treat us badly'.[3]

Of course, that is not the whole picture. Many of God's people do care for their ministers. What is more, in spite of the difficulties, most ministers gain enormous satisfaction. 29 per cent of ministers felt very satisfied in ministry, with a further per cent satisfied[4] Indeed, in a 2014 UK Government survey on job satisfaction 'clergy' topped the list of 274 occupations![5] Although ministry can be very tough, it can also very rewarding.

This dual aspect of ministry was very apparent in a survey of retired Baptist ministers I undertook in 2018. In reply to the question 'Did you have a good experience of ministry?', almost three quarters (72 per cent) said: 'For the most part it was rewarding, but there were tough times'.[6] In the reply to the question, 'If you had an opportunity to begin life again, would you want to be a minister?', over half (57 per cent) said without qualification that if they had such an opportunity, they would want to be a minister again. But this positivity did not negate the fact that some experienced very tough times. These low points of ministry were varied. However, the issues mentioned by the respondents were overwhelmingly 'politics and power struggles; conflict and

---

[2] *Power for God's Sake*, 104.
[3] *Power for God's Sake*, 106.
[4] *Power for God's Sake*, 36.
[5] See 'Vicar or publican – which jobs make you happy?' *BBC News Magazine* (25/04/2014).
[6] *Retirement Matters for Ministers*, 51.

dissension; manipulation, criticism, gossip, back-biting, resistance to change and resulting opposition; bullying and aggression from deacons; breakdown of relationships with other members of a staff team; misunderstanding and rejection'.

As a result, some ministers felt they had to resign, while others were sacked; yet others had to take time off work. The in-depth interviews I conducted with seventeen individual ministers revealed an amazing amount of trauma and pain. As I said in my report, 'To my surprise, I discovered that each one of them, in their own different way, was a hero of faith'.[7]

There are times when ministry is tough, but those tough times are well and truly outweighed by the good times. Along with the low points mentioned by the retired ministers in my survey, there were also the high points. Repeatedly my respondents commented on:

- seeing people young and old coming to faith
- the joy of baptising new Christians
- experiencing church growth
- leading worship
- presiding at the Lord's Table
- preaching every Sunday to the same people
- pastoral visiting and care
- being part of people's lives
- taking dedications, weddings and funerals
- developing church premises
- working with others.[8]

As I look back on my own ministry, I feel incredibly blessed. As a missionary in Africa, as a minister of two churches in England, and as a principal of a theological college, I have had a wonderful life. There were tough times: my principalship at Spurgeon's College did not end happily, and the first seven years of my ministry in Chelmsford were fraught with difficulty. Yet, for the most part ministry for me has been almost embarrassingly rewarding.

After almost fifty years of ministry, I believe that being called to be a minister of a church is the most wonderful calling in the

---

[7] *Retirement Matters for Ministers*, 16.
[8] *Retirement Matters for Ministers*, 52.

world. Unfortunately, some ministers forget how privileged they are. Just on a very basic level,

- What a privilege it is to be paid by God's people to serve God in his church full-time! Some of those we have served would have given their right arm to do so. Many people in our churches have pretty mundane jobs, whereas we have been able to focus on things that really matter.
- What a privilege too it has been to enter into people's homes and to share with them in some of the happiest and saddest times in their lives! Rightly understood pastoral visiting is not a chore, but a wonderful opportunity to represent the Lord Jesus to all and sundry.
- What a privilege it has been to be given time to study God's Word day by day, and then on a Sunday to be able to share the fruits of that study with God's people. True it is a demanding task coming up with something fresh Sunday by Sunday, but what a great calling is ours to share the good news of Jesus.
- What a privilege it has been to be surrounded by the many 'ordinary' people in our churches who loved us, encouraged us, prayed for us, and showed so many kindnesses to us! Add to that too the many people who gave so freely of their time to serve us as elders or deacons or church wardens or church stewards.

Then there were all those special highlights of ministry: the excitement of Christmas Day and the thrill of many an Easter Sunday morning. The days when the church was packed for a baptismal service, for a wedding and even for a funeral. As God's man or God's woman, we have been privileged to be at the centre of people's evolving lives.

In many ways I would love to start all over again as a minister of Christ -not least because with all the wisdom and experience I have experienced I could now do a better job! Sadly, however, I would not then have the same energy. But as it is God has called me to continue to serve him in retirement, and that is a privilege. It has been – and remains – a most rewarding calling.

MINISTRY IS ROOTED
IN THE GRACE OF GOD

*A draft of a sermon to be preached at Chelmsford Cathedral at a special
service of Evensong on Sunday 11 October 2020:*

On Saturday evening 10 October 1970 at the age of 25 I was
ordained to the Christian ministry. Now here I am a lifetime later:
43 years were spent in stipendiary ministry, followed by seven years
of active retirement. For me ministry did not end when I retired.
I may no longer run a church, but God still has a call on my life.

I could never have dreamt where God would take me over
these 50 years. To my surprise my ministry began in Congo, where
for two years I served with the BMS, teaching Greek and New
Testament in the Protestant Theological Faculty of what became the
National University of Zaire. Then came 13 years as the minister
of Altrincham Baptist Church, Cheshire; 6 years as Principal of
Spurgeon's College, London; and 21 years as minister of Central
Baptist Church, Chelmsford. Nor could I have ever dreamt that
Caroline and I would end up as members of an Anglican Cathedral.

When I retired in March 2014, Central Baptist Church,
Chelmsford, put on a farewell service at which many kind things
were said about me. Today's service, however, is very different in
character. Instead of celebrating Paul Beasley-Murray, I want this
service to be a celebration of the grace of God – God's undeserved
favour on my life. There are times when I almost feel guilty –
why should God have blessed me in this way. As I wrote in my
autobiography, *This is my Story*:

> 'As I look back over my life, there is so much for which I am
> grateful—and for which I thank God:

1. I thank God for his amazing love for me seen above all in Jesus. What a difference Jesus makes to living (and, of course, to dying too).

2. I thank God for the family in which I grew up, and for the love and security which they gave me.

3. I thank God for Caroline and for the family which is now ours, and for the love and support that I have received from them.

4. I thank God for the many friends who have enriched our lives, as also for those friends who are still there for us.

5. I thank God for the privilege of having been a pastor. It is undoubtedly the most wonderful calling in the world.

6. I thank God for so much happiness and fulfilment in ministry; I thank God even for the tough times, because they have brought about a depth and maturity which otherwise I would not have had.

7. I thank God for the new freedoms and opportunities of 'retirement'.

8. I thank God for the many undeserved blessings of life, such as health and strength, opportunities to travel and see so much of the world, and the resources to enjoy so many of the good things of life. In the words of the Psalmist 'the lines have fallen for me in pleasant places' (Ps 16:6). God has been good in the way in which he has 'marked out' the parameters of my life.'[1]

Today three Scriptures come to mind.

Firstly, 1 Sam. 7:12 where the prophet Samuel celebrates a famous victory over the Philistines, by setting up a stone: 'He named it "Ebenezer" (i.e. Stone of Help), for he said, "Thus far the Lord has helped us".' John Goldingay in his commentary noted that 'helping' can have a variety of connotations. It can be used of giving a person a 'helping hand' – that simply makes life a little easier. However, at the battle of Mizpah the help God gave made all the difference. Without him the Israelites would have been defeated.

---

[1] Paul Beasley-Murray, *This Is My Story*, 201

'Helping" here 'is not so different from 'delivering'. It is something God does when you cannot help yourself.'[2] Today, on this special anniversary of my ordination I want to mark the occasion by celebrating the grace of God over these past fifty years.

In the words of Robert Robinson's great hymn, 'Come Thou Fount of every blessing',[3] I too want to say

> *'Here I raise my Ebenezer,*
> *Hither by they help I've come'.*

And with Robinson I too want to declare

> *'O to grace how great a debtor*
> *Daily I'm constrained to be.'*

Secondly,1 Cor. 15:10 where the Apostle Paul reflected on his ministry: 'But by the grace of God I am what I am, and his grace towards me has not been in vain. On the contrary, I worked harder than any of them (viz the 12 apostles to whom the risen Lord had appeared) – though it was not I, but the grace of God that is with me.' Here Paul celebrated the grace of God -in triplicate. Three times in one verse he speaks of the grace of God: 'by the grace of God I am what I am'; 'his grace towards me has not been in vain'; and he attributes his achievements to 'the grace of God that is with me'.

What I find significant is the contrast Paul made between God's grace and his own sense of identity, his own ego. Yes, ego is the word. 'Not I' (literally 'not ego'). *But* (Paul uses two adversatives) the grace of God'. Paul had good reason to boast. In the words of F.F. Bruce, my PhD supervisor, and at the time the Rylands Professor of Biblical Criticism and Exegesis in the University of Manchester: 'Latecomer as he was to the apostolate, he strove to make up for lost time and the sum-total of his achievements thus far surpassed the record of those who had been called earlier. The extent of these achievements is impressive enough, even if we go no farther back than the six or seven years immediately preceding the writing of this letter: he had evangelised the process of Galatia,

---

[2] John Goldingay, *1 & 2 Samuel for Everyone* (SPCK, London, 2011). 41.
[3] Robert Robinson (1735-1790), Come thou fount of every blessing', *The Baptist Hymn Book* (Psalms & Hymns Trust, London 1962), Hymn Number 494.

Macedonia and Achaia, and was not actively engaged in evangelising proconsular Asia ... Yet all the credit is ascribed to 'the grace of God' which called him ... and made him what he was.'[4] For Paul, all the hard work which lay behind his achievements was not the result of a personal need to compensate God for his grace but were a reflection of God's grace at work in his life. All was of grace.

Finally, John 15:5: 'Apart from me', said Jesus, 'you can do nothing'. This means, said William Temple, 'All fruit that I ever bear or can bear comes wholly from his life within me. No particle of it is mine as distinct from his. There is, no doubt, some part of his whole purpose that He would accomplish through me; that is my work, my fruit, in the sense that I, and not another, am the channel of his life for this end; but in no other sense. Whatever has its ultimate origin in myself is sin.'[5]

From start to finish ministry is rooted in the grace of God. However gifted and skilled ministers may be, however hard-working and committed they may be, ultimately we are dependent upon the grace of God at work in our lives. To God – and to God alone – be the glory!

---

[4] F. F. Bruce, *1 & 2 Corinthians: New Century Bible* (Oliphants, London, 1971), 143.
[5] William Temple, *Readings in St John's Gospel* (Macmillan edition, London, 1963), 251.

APPENDIX

Disciple and Teacher, Servant and Master

Notes of a sermon preached by George Raymond Beasley-Murray
on the occasion of the ordination of his son, Paul Beasley-Murray.
Saturday 10 October 1970

While going through the papers of my late father, I came across the notes of the sermon my father preached at my own ordination. I found it quite a spiritual tonic to read them. I confess that I had totally forgotten what he had said at the time. With the passing of the years I realise how apt the sermon was for me. I have refrained from re-casting the notes into inclusive language – things were different in 1970.

'A disciple is not above his teacher, nor a servant above his master. It is enough for the disciple to be like his teacher, and the servant like his master.' (Matt. 10:24)

Observe the terms: The disciple is sent out to be a teacher. But he always remains a disciple – a learner. The servant is sent in the name of his master – and he always remains a servant. This is how Jesus went – always learning from his Father, always obedient to his Father.

First, the disciple shares the reproach of his teacher, the servant shares the rejection of his master. See Matt. 10:32: 'If they have called the master of the house Beelzebub, how much more will they malign those of his household'. That Jesus should ever have been called Beelzebub was the most shocking instance of the total rejection he suffered at the hands of the religious leaders of his time. Jesus was a tool of the devil! The spirit in him was the power of evil. Therefore everything for which he stood was to be rejected as abhorrent. This led him to the grave words about blasphemy

211

against the Holy Spirit. If Jesus should suffer such rejection, how much more will his disciples know it? See John 15:20. Basic to the message of Jesus and integral to the experience of the early disciples is the inevitability of the disciple sharing his master's fate: see Matt. 5:11,12; Luke 9:57ff.; Mark 8:34; Mark 13:10. The sermons of the Book of Acts are chiefly delivered in hostile surroundings. The missionary progress of the Church through the ages is marked by the blood stains of its heralds. Recognise the inevitability of hardship as a minister of Christ. It is in this that his partnership is learned and experienced.

Second, the disciple shares the attitude of his teacher, the servant shares that of his master. And that is a love which stoops to the lowliest and costliest service. See John 13:16: 'I have given you an example that you should do as I have done for you. A servant is not greater than his master, nor is he who is sent greater than he who sent him. If you know these things, happy are you if you do them.' The first implication of this statement: preparedness for menial service. Foot-washing was the slave's job! The humility of Christ is to be expressed in readiness for work that only a 'Christly' man would do. The second implication: preparedness for sacrificial self-giving for the salvation of the world. See Phil. 2:6-8 and v.5. No doubt this is for the whole Church and not for the minister alone (Phil. 2:5 addressed to the church). But the minister must lead his people in this kind of ministry, and set them an example. It is unthinkable to tell people to walk in the steps of Jesus, and stand back. The servant church requires the servant leaders to show them the mind of the servant of the Lord.

Third, the disciple shares his teacher's success, the servant shares his master's glory. See John 15:20: 'If they kept my word, they will keep yours also'. Light in the darkness! The power and blessing of God that was with Jesus is with the disciples of Jesus. See also Luke 6:40: 'A disciple is not above his teacher, but everyone when he is fully taught will be like his teacher'. This is in contrast to the terrible results of the blind leading the blind: he who knows the truth of Jesus will be able to lead them into the power of that truth just as Jesus did. This is the joyful, reverse side of the principle enunciated by Jesus. If men rejected him, men also listened to him. Even on the cross. And especially through the cross. See